# THE PATHOLOGY OF NORMALCY

# The Pathology of Normalcy

Erich Fromm
Edited by Rainer Funk

ISBN: 979-8-3372-0915-9

This edition published in 2026 by Open Road Integrated Media, Inc.
180 Maiden Lane
New York, NY 10038
www.openroadmedia.com

# CONTENTS

# THE PATHOLOGY OF NORMALCY

## I. Modern Man's Pathology of Normalcy

Four lectures given 1953 at the New School of Social Research in New York

# 1. MENTAL HEALTH IN THE MODERN WORLD

## (FIRST LECTURE: JANUARY 26, 1953)

### a) What is mental health?

There are two possible approaches to the question of what is mental health in contemporary society. One is statistical and one is an analytical, qualitative approach.

The statistical one is simple and can be talked about briefly. Here one asks what are the figures of mental health in modern society, what do the statistics say. These figures are indeed not terribly encouraging. We hear that we spent per year about one billion dollars for the care of mental sickness in the United States, and that about half of our hospital beds are being occupied by mentally sick patients.

These figures are even a little less encouraging, and kind of bewildering and even suggestive, if we consider some data on Europe, where we find that the countries in Europe, which are the most well-balanced, middle-class secure countries, like Switzerland, Sweden, Denmark and Finland belong to those countries which have the poorest mental health, that is to say, a great deal more schizophrenics, suicide, alcoholism and manslaughter than the other European countries.

Here our statistical data really poses a problem. What does it mean that those European countries, who have achieved socially and culturally exactly what seems to be an ideal we are striving for and have not as yet achieved that rather prosperous, middle class existence based on a great deal of economic security and yet that these countries seem to have a state of mental health which does not prove that this kind of existence is as conducive to mental health or to happiness, as we always believed.

At the same time, while there is a great deal of mental illness in the United States and in Europe, on the other side of the ledger, there are many good things which can be said. We have increasing care for mentally sick patients. We have developed new methods. We have a mental hygiene movement in Europe and America, and we don't know really, do our figures simply reflect a greater amount of mental illness or do they indirectly reflect a greater care for mental health, namely that by better methods, more accurate observation, larger facilities, we recognize much more who is mentally sick and therefore our statistics are much worse than they would be if we did not have this attention and focus on mental health and sickness. I think if we just follow the statistical approach and look at the figures on one side of the ledger and the other, we would be just as confused as before we had the figures and wouldn't know what they meant, which is often the case when we only look at statistics.

I should like to discuss in these four lectures not the statistical side but the qualitative side. To start out with the question "What do we mean by mental health and mental sickness?"—and then to discuss the question: "How are the facts of mental health and sickness as we describe them related to the particular structure of our culture as of the year 1953?" If we want to speak of mental health in contemporary culture, we have not only to compare mental health on the one side and our culture on the other as a fixed point, but we have to understand the implications, what in the procedure, what in the structure makes for elements which are conducive to health, and what in the structure makes for elements conducive to mental sickness.

If we ask what do we mean by mental health, we have to differentiate between two basic concepts which are still current, and often not clearly differentiated, although the difference is quite clear. One is a relativistic, social concept. It corresponds to the state of mind which the majority of society have. That is about like the definition of intelligence. Intelligence is what is measured by an intelligence test. Mental health from that standpoint is adjustment to the ways of life of an existing society quite regardless of whether this society as such is healthy or crazy. All that matters is that the person is adjusted to it.

Many of you know the story of H. G. Wells, *The Country of the Blind* (1925), where a young man who gets somehow lost in Malaya, comes to a tribe where people for generations are all congenitally blind. He sees. That is bad luck because they are all very suspicious and there are very learned doctors who diagnose his illness as a strange or unheard of disturbance in his face, which produces all sorts of strange and pathological phenomena: ["Those queer things that are called the eyes, and which exist to make an agreeable soft depression in the face, are diseased in his case in such a way as to affect his brain. They are greatly distended, he has eyelashes, and his eyelids move, and consequently his brain is in a state of constant irritation and distraction."] He falls in love with a girl there, and the father is reluctant, but finally is willing to permit the marriage if the young man would consent to an operation which make him blind. But before he gives permission to be blinded, he runs away.

The implication of Wells, in a sense, is simple enough, that is more or less what we all feel about normal and not normal, health and sickness, if we speak from the standpoint of adjustment. Now there, are certain underlying assumptions in the principle of adjustment. The assumption is, every society as such, is normal, and secondly, mental illness is deviation from what is the personality type which this society wants, and thirdly, the aim of mental hygiene, the aim of psychiatry, the aim of psychotherapy, is to restore man to the ways of the average personality, regardless of whether they are blind or he is blind. What matters is that he is adjusted and that they are not disturbed.

In this standpoint, there are certain elements which can be distinguished. One is the feeling element: We are all prone to believe that our family, our nation, our race are normal and that the ways of the others are not normal. Maybe I can tell a joke which makes this point rather drastically, of a man who goes to the doctor and wants to tell him some symptom of his, so he starts his story by saying: "Well, Doctor, every morning, after I have taken a shower and after I have vomited," and the Doctor says: "What, you mean you vomit every morning?" and the patient says: "But Doctor, doesn't everybody do that?"

I think it is rather funny because it just emphasizes an attitude which we all have more or less. We may know that our most peculiar idiosyncrasies are shared by others, but we do not know that there are many idiosyncrasies which we consider the common property of mankind which are rather peculiar to our families, the United States, or the Western world in general, but which are by no means necessary parts of the structure of humanity.

But there is not only a feeling involved, a provincial feeling that the way we are and the way we are brought up is normal.

There is also a philosophy involved. The philosophy is what you might call the relativistic philosophy which says in the first place: "There are no objectively valid value statements which can be made." Good and bad are matters of faith, if you please. They are essentially nothing but the expression of what is done and preferred in one culture as against the other. What people in one culture like to do, they call good and what they don't like to do, they call bad. But there is nothing objective about it. This is nothing but a matter of taste.

In contrast to this standpoint is another one, which I have dealt with more in detail in *Man for Himself* [E Fromm, 1947a], which makes the assumption that there are indeed value judgments which are objectively valid, and not matters of taste and also not matters of faith. Just as the doctor or physiologist can make an objectively valid statement that provided we begin with one axiom and that is, that to live is better than to die, or life is better than death, then indeed this food is better than another one. This kind of air, or rest or amount of sleep is better than another one. One is good for health. The other one is bad for the health of the person. I believe that, not only with regard to our body, but, if you please, with regard to our soul too, we can make an equally objective statement about what is good and what is bad for our soul, based on whatever knowledge we have about its nature and about laws which govern it.

We know indeed very little. We know perhaps more about vitamins and calories than we know about that which our psyche needs in order to live normally, but then fashions change with regard to vitamins and calories, as we have all experienced, and I don't know whether, if we took the problem more seriously, the problem of our soul, we might not discover that we have a good deal of knowledge about it, if we only pay attention to it.

This sociological relativism which says: "That which is necessary for the existence and survival of a specific society, is also that which is good in itself," is not as arbitrary as it sounds. In fact, from the standpoint of any existing society, one can hardly see how it could fail to take this attitude, because a society of a specific structure can exist only inasmuch as its members adopt an attitude which guarantees more or less smooth functioning of this society. One of the great efforts which every society makes, in its cultural institutions, educational institutions, religious ideas and so on, is to create a type of personality which wants to do what he has to do, which is not only willing, but eager to fulfill that role which is required in that society, so that it can function smoothly.

If you take a warrior—like predatory society, in which the function of the members in the social group is to make war, to conquer, to be aggressive, to steal to kill, and you find there one member who corresponds, more or less to Ferdinand the Bull, in this society they would be quite hampered in making war and continuing that structure. This structure is after all not the result of some arbitrary choice, but is rooted in a great number of objective historic conditions, in which that society functions, and which cannot be changed so easily. Or. if you took, on the other hand, the cooperative, agricultural society, and you find one member of this society who was a warrior type, he would be equally disturbed. He would be considered equally sick, and if more people could develop in that way, they would be a threat to the functioning of that society.

You might say, every functioning society has a vested, a legitimate interest, in a certain amount of conformity, an interest from the standpoint of the survival of this society, that has to satisfy its own structure and social individuality. This expectation of conforming is stressed in life. Certainly there is no need for me, in the year 1953, to stress conformity, but maybe what needs to be stressed a little more, is that the survival of the society, at least of modern society, is also based on the fact of non-conformity. If the society of cave-dwellers existed on the basis of complete conformity, we still would be living in caves quite obviously, and we would still be cannibals.

One might say that the development of mankind depends on the fact that there is a certain willingness to conform, and a certain willingness, eagerness not to conform, and that, not only for the development of progress, but indeed for the survival of any society of the human race, the willingness not to conform is as essential for the society itself, as a certain willingness to conform, and to adjust to the rules in which this society plays the game of life.

In these various views about normal being the same as adjusted, or health being the same as adjustment, you find eventually another position which I am afraid is mostly a rationalization. This position says: "No, I am not a relativist. I am not saying every society is living according to what is normal and good and healthy, but it just happens that our society—the American society in the year 1953, the American way of life—happens to be the end and fulfillment of human aspiration." That is the way in which normal people live, and while other societies up to now, or up to the last 150 years were backward, perhaps abnormal, did things which were not right, we are at the point where the basic of life, of our society, coincides with that which from an objective and not from a relativist standpoint is to be called "normal" and "healthy."

That is indeed a very dangerous standpoint because while it sounds so objective, and while it sounds different from a sociological relativist position, actually it is only another way of rationalizing the same thing without saying so. I shall spend some time in trying to show that while there are many good points in our society, many things if one wants, to be proud of, that it is at least very questionable whether the way of life in which we live right now is more conducive to mental health or to mental illness.

What I want to do in these lectures is to analyze more concretely the effect of our way of life on man. What does it do to man, the way we live, the way our society is organized, the way we are organized politically? What does it do to our mental health, to what extent is it conductive to mental illness and what are the various reactions and possibilities to go on from there, to make that which is good better and that which is bad disappear.

I realize that in the year 1953, things are a little emotional. On the one hand, you find a criticism of the United States which today you really only find with the Stalinists, in which you hear that people not only are starving all over the country, there is nothing good and everything is bad. This is a kind of criticism which is not to be taken with too much concern, at least from any objective standpoint, because it is just a lie. I think that the world in which we live right here is one of the best worlds the human race ever developed, which isn't saying so much, because so far, the human race has not developed such good worlds, and I have a lot to criticize about it, at least from the standpoint of observing what goes on. But nevertheless, this is my first reaction when I hear that this is such a terrible world because if one is acquainted with what has gone on in the world in the last five, six thousand years, one may say, this is, in spite of everything, one of the best experiments which have been made so far, and with all its terrific shortcomings, it is something which gives hope for a very constructive development, provided we have the sense to see what is necessary and to avoid things which can be avoided.

On the other extreme is the patriotic approach which says the American way of life is all that can be wished for. It is the best that ever existed and there are no questions to be asked. That is a rather primitive standpoint which does not show much thought, and I am afraid not even much concern, because I don't see any reason why it should be a kind of virtue to think my country is wonderful when we all think it is not a virtue to say I am wonderful. If I run around saying I am just wonderful, you will think I am rather strange, and you will not have too much respect for me, but if I say my country is wonderful, that is supposed to be very wise and it is supposed to be virtuous. It is an expression of real egocentricity, and the same lack of concern, if one is satisfied to make these statements without inquiring about what is wrong and being concerned with it.

## b) Principles and attitudes of modern society

Before we go into the concrete problem of mental health in contemporary society, let me discuss very briefly what are the basic principles and attitudes on which modern society is based, in which it is rooted.

The first principle of the modern Western world is that an individual emerges from a group to which he belongs in a fixed and prescribed manner and has to live and to fit more himself, that he emerges as an individual and is not any more a member of a static society, as the feudal society of the Middle Ages was for many centuries. This is, in a sense, what we call the individualism or freedom of modern man, as against the fixed position, the static position of medieval man who was primarily a member of a group and by the very nature of this structure never ceased to be a member of this group. Modern man has emerged from these primary ties, from these original structures. But—and I shall add a but in all of these points, which I am trying to make now—but he is afraid of the freedom he achieved. He is not a member of an organic group any more, but he has become an automaton who then, in a secondary fashion holds on to society, to convention, to public opinion, to all sorts of groupings, because he doesn't know what to do with his freedom. He cannot stand it to be alone and free from these earlier ties in which his place was given and determined by society.

Another feature of modern Western society closely related to that of the emerging of the individual from this collective organization of society, is what is usually called "individual initiative." Let us say, in the medieval guild, the member of the guild was dependent in his economic activity on the guild. In modern capitalist society people are free. The capitalist is free. The worker is free. They strike out for themselves and they develop each, that which one calls "individual initiative." However, with all that individual initiative which was so pronounced in the nineteenth century, we live actually in a culture where people have less and less individual initiative, that is to say, they may have individual initiative in an economic sense, but even that is much less than it used to be a hundred years ago because of certain changes in the structure of modern capitalism. But if you question what the individual initiative is in anything else besides how to invest your money, it is indeed very little, if we get down to the point.

Perhaps people in the medieval society had as much or more individual initiative, if we refer by that to the surprise of living, to taking life as an adventure, to making something out of it, to differ a little bit from my neighbor. I say that probably people in most cultures have more individual initiative than we have. I think individual initiative in a human sense, as differentiated from a purely economic sense, is at a very low ebb in modern man.

The third feature, characteristic of modern society, is that we have created a science and an activity which has permitted us to combat, to master nature to an unheard of degree—which is all perfectly true. But we—the proud people who started out to dominate nature—have become slaves of the very economic machine which we created in the process. We dominated nature, but our machine dominates us. We are perhaps more dominated by the artifacts we have created with our machines, than in many cultures people are dominated by nature which they have not learned to master. At least, if you consider the danger of earthquakes or a flood, which are dangers of nature, and to compare these dangers with the risk of an atomic war, then I think that it is a symbol of how we are threatened by our own production in a way much more than cultures which are dominated by nature.

The fourth characteristic of modern culture is its scientific approach. By scientific approach I mean something which goes far beyond the technical sense of what is a scientific approach. The scientific approach, humanly speaking, is an ability to be objective, that is to say to have the humility to see the world as it is, or other people, other things and ourselves, and not to distort the reality by our wishes and our feelings, to have faith in the power of our thought for recognizing the truth, the reality, but to be willing all the time to change the results of our thinking by new data which we find, and by being honest and objective in not avoiding data which we might find in order to avoid changing our own picture.

The modern scientific approach is, I would say, humanly speaking, one of the greatest steps in human progress because it signifies the expression of a spirit of humility, objectivity, realism, which does not in the same degree and in the same manner exist in those cultures in which the scientific approach does not exist. But what have we done with it? We are now worshippers of science and have made scientific statement the substitute for old religious dogmas. The scientific approach is for us not at all an expression of that humility or objectivity, but it is just another formulation of a dogma. The average person believes that the scientist is a priest who knows all the answers and who is in direct touch with all that he wants to know, just as some people are satisfied that the priest, if he is in touch with God, if he can see him once in a while he feels he has some part in this communication with God. So if you read "Popular Science," and know the latest discoveries, and are convinced that there are scientists who know all the answers, you participate in this new dogma, the religion of science, and you have never to do any thinking for yourself.

Another feature of contemporary civilization of the last two hundred years is our political democracy, also a tremendous step forward. It means that people can decide not only about how their taxes are used, but also about all important issues in society. They can decide for themselves. But again you might say this idea and this principle which originally was a reaction to the principle of the absolute state or even the feudal state, where people had no right to participate in the decisions about their own lives, has deteriorated in many ways if I would use a very strong expression, to betting on the horse-track, with all the excitement, all the risk-taking, all the irrational elements that number three might be the right horse because I dreamt of it last night. While I don't deny there is a certain amount of rationality in our voting process on the whole it cannot be described as a thoughtful concern of individuals in the affairs of society. I still think it is better than anything else we have but certainly it is far from what was originally formulated.

You might ask, is there something common to all these new factors in modern society as I tried to describe them, namely that they have to be understood, in the first place as negations of the pre-modern structure. Individual freedom, individual enterprise, the scientific approach, political democracy, the domination of nature, all these are primarily expressed in terms of negation. It is the opposite. It is different. It is a negation of those points in the feudal structure, but I am afraid we are getting stuck with a negation that we still formulate and conceive of these ideas in terms of a negation which was new two or three hundred years ago, rather than to come to a new level of discourse, to, if you please, a negation of the negation, a critical appraisal of what this negation means, or you might say, that we go beyond the negation and come to new, more positive formulations of what we want. Because after all, feudalism or even the absolute state, is not our problem any more. While an editorial of the *New York Times* may have been the most revealing and heartening and suggestive document a hundred years ago, I cannot find that in 1953 the editorials have this effect on me, and I don't think that they have this effect on anyone else except perhaps of confirming what he thinks, which is always a nice and pleasant experience.

On the whole I think if we consider the positive features of our culture and our society, we should recognize that we are still stuck in the negations that it is a little late for that. It is a long time since the negation really was fruitful and constructive, and we should arrive from the negation to a new level which is either the negation of the negation, or you might formulate it, as let us say, a new position.

## c) Human conditions and psychic needs

Before I come to the discussion of what the effect of our social and cultural structure is on man, and on the mental health, I should like to make some more general statements which are necessary in order to explain my approach. Let me begin with a statement that it is necessary for every individual to give an answer to the problem of his existence. There is a general assumption that if we have enough to eat or to drink, and enough sleep and enough security, and as Freud would add, a normal sexual satisfaction, if all this is given and not disturbed, that then life is no particular problem. But the point is, that then the problems begin.

It is true enough if you haven't enough to eat, if you have insecurity and difficulty in the most basic levels of life, then indeed you have problems, but you haven't even started to touch the real problems of human existence. May I come back to some of the figures from the well-balanced Protestant small countries of Europe. They have solved most of their problems on that level. They have enough to eat. They have cooperation. They have no fierce competition. They have not even participated in a war. But there is an amount of secret boredom doing on in this kind of life which leads to explosive results in terms of mental health.

We speak so often of the evils of life; sickness, mental illness, alcoholism, what not, but I think we are not sufficiently aware that one of the worst sufferings in life is boredom and that people go to any lengths and any effort, not to avoid it because that is not too easy, but to escape it, to cover it up. In fact, you might say there are eight hours a day in which we are not bored because we work hard and we are grateful that God has given us a need to sleep which fills out anther eight hours, but our greatest problem is how to fill the other eight hours and how to cope with the boredom which is constantly aroused in our way of living.

The human situation is characterized by profound dichotomies and contradictions. The most basic one—the one of the limitation of our existence which in the last analysis is expressed by the necessity of death—has to do with the fact that we are part of the animal world in our whole physiological organization, and at the same time, are free of the animal world, that we before to it, in it, and in the same time, don't belong to it. We have reason and imagination which permit us and almost force us to be aware of ourselves as distinct, separate entities, and of our end which is unavoidable, and which is the very opposite of life.

We are confronted with these contradictions in our existence, and we have to make some sense of our life. We just cannot stand living, merely eating and drinking and not making sense. We have to give some answer to the problem of living and we have to give some answers theoretically and practically. By this I mean that we need a frame of reference in which we orient ourselves in life, which makes the process of living and our position in it somehow sensible and meaningful. Unless we are crazy, or unless we repress, as some people do, and many people can do it almost completely, the awareness of the problems of existence by following compulsively a routine of escape, we are bothered with the question of the meaning of life and we need some frame of reference and orientation, which makes sense. This is not only an intellectual frame of reference, but we need also an organizing principle of an object of devotion, of something to which we devote our energies beyond those which we need for producing and reproducing.

You might say: Is this not perfectly axiomatic? How can one

prove it? I don't know whether I can prove it to anyone's satisfaction. All I can say is that from observing myself, and that is where one should always start, from observing other people who seek psychiatric help, and from observing what goes on in the world, I have the impression that this need of a frame of reference which gives meaning, and this need of an object of devotion which permits us to focus our powers on something which goes beyond the process of physical production of the things we need in order to stay alive, that these two needs are imperative needs and nobody can avoid them. In this sense we all need religion, provided we use the definition of religion in a very general sense, namely a system of orientation and object of devotion, regardless of what the specific contents are. In this sense, and from the standpoint of this definition, of course we would not only speak of theistic religion as we are accustomed to the Western world, but Buddhism, Confucius, Taoism and in the same sense, Stalinism or Fascism because it appeals to those needs in man which refer to that which in our culture a religion satisfies.

## d) Mental health and the need for religion

There are many answers which one can give to the problems of existence. In fact, if you take even a simple text book on the history of religion, you will find probably all the answers to the problem of human existence which have been given so far, because the various religions are various answers to the same problem. If you read a textbook of psychopathology and study neuroses and psychoses, you would find that neuroses and psychoses are more individual answers which people have given to the problem of existence and very often those people suffer from neuroses and psychoses who are more sensitive in their quest for something meaningful than perhaps the majority, who have the thicker skins, in whom the quest, you might say, the religious quest in this sense, for a specific frame of reference, for some specific object of devotion is in terms of what your culture orders, that because of their greater sensitivity or because of a less easily neglected demand for this, they develop their prophet religion and the psychiatrist calls it a neurosis or psychosis.

I wonder sometimes whether a person has to become insane these days in order to feel certain things. Lessing once said: "Who doesn't become insane over certain things, has no sanity to lose," which is all pretty much the same point, and I am afraid we are all glib, or at least psychiatrists are very glib to judge what is neurotic, what is insane, from a standpoint which again assumes that our way of feeling, our experiences or answers to the problems of existence, are pretty much what a person ought to be satisfied with. Therefore, if he isn't and develops a more profound or peculiar system of orientation and devotion, if you please, then he is simply considered to be insane, neurotic.

I don't mean to say, that all insane people are really saints and inspired by God, as some primitive cultures believe. I think there is something to be said for the modern differentiation between sanity and insanity, but I am not that impressed by the certainty with which this statement is made. You probably know the joke which many doctors and patients make in some mental hospitals, that the only difference between the doctor and the patient is who has the key. I think that just is a good way of expressing that there is some room for doubt about all our definitions of what is sane, what is insane, what is neurotic, what is normal. All these definition are based on the assumption that the normal part of our population has found a perfectly satisfactory answer to the problem of human existence, and anyone who is not capable of accepting this answer gracefully or graciously, or who seeks for some peculiar solution is sick and nothing but sick.

Religion in this broad sense of the definition—as need for a system of orientation—is something peculiar to all men in one form or another. I should like to add, the choice is not at all between religion or no religion, provided we use the term in this general sense. The choice is only between a good religion and a bad religion, or a better religion or a worse. Or to put it differently, we are all "idealists:" We are prompted by motives which go beyond our self-interest. This "idealism" is the greatest blessing, but it is also the greatest curse. There is hardly anything men have ever done harmful to the world, which has not been done out of sheer idealism—"idealism" again defined now not in terms of any specific context, but of those strivings transcending beyond the routine task of continuing our life and of surviving, and of creating a frame of reference and an object of devotion which goes beyond and transcends our biological survival.

To say that somebody is an "idealist" as an excuse is just stupid. We all are. The only question is what are our ideals. Are we driven by the wish to destroy, to dominate, to control, to strangle life, which is just as much "idealism" psychologically speaking, in this sense of my definition, as it would be if we are driven by a wish for love, cooperation. The only question is: Are we dangerous or are we good for the world? But we can only discuss the question meaningfully if we refer to it in the context and aim of the specific religion or ideal we have rather than to a statement that some people are idealistic and some are not.

We have seen and still see in some countries in the world that people succeed in impressing others with the very fact that they are idealists, and therefore giving dignity to the hellish things they are doing. We still have the strange notion that it is good to be idealistic, rather than to say that that is to be taken for granted. We all are, and there is nothing particularly desirable about it because we can't help it. We are driven to be. The only question is to get over the admiration for idealism and religion and all that, and to ask the only pertinent question. What are your aims? What are the goals? What are the effects? What frame of reference have you in your ideal?

Naturally, if we can speak right now of good and bad religion, of good and bad ideals, we come back to the question I touched upon in the beginning: Are there any objectively valid value judgments which can be made? Even at the risk of being called completely unscientific and dogmatic, I want simply to state what I consider to be objective and valid aims for mental health. I am sorry that what I say is extremely old, and there is not one new word in it, because while I might employ some fancy scientific language, I prefer to use old words which have some meaning, which all of us, or at least the scientists among us, shy away from today.

What I mean to say is that the *aim of life* which corresponds to the nature of man in his situation of existence, is to be able to love, to be able to use one's reason and to be able to have the objectivity and humility to be in touch with a reality outside of oneself, inside of oneself, without leading to distortion. This type of relatedness to the world is the greatest source of energy beyond that produced by the chemistry of the body. There is nothing more conducive to creating anything than love as far as it is genuine. Being in touch with reality, doing away with fiction, having the humility and objectivity to see what is, and not talk about things which separate us from reality, is the most essential basis for any sense of security, for any sense of feeling "I" without needing props which substitute for that feeling of identity.

I think that while one might not be able to prove conclusively that these are the aims which all religions profess, they are the aims of most great religions. They are not, for that reason, simply metaphysical aims springing from faith, although they are those aims proclaimed by almost all great religions in the last five thousand years. Modern anthropology and psychopathology and psychology can show that by studying the nature of man, by studying the problems of human existence, one can find, with as much empirical evidence as we have for the usefulness of vitamins that these are the aims which make for the best and only satisfactory solution of the complex problems of living and existence.

# 2. THE FRAME OF REFERENCE AND DEVOTION IN CONTEMPORARY CULTURE

# (SECOND LECTURE: JANUARY 28, 1953)

## a) The religious vacuum

I had been speaking last time about the need for a frame of reference and an object of devotion as a general and basic human need, which is normally satisfied in a culture by what we usually call "religion."

What do we see about this frame of reference and devotion in contemporary culture? By contemporary culture, I mean modern development since the end of the Middle Ages. We might say that in modern society the end of the religious culture of the Middle Ages led to what we might call a religious vacuum. The feudal order of religion has not been replaced by anything, and what we witness is a growing vacuum in the sense of a religious frame of reference, of an object of devotion.

We see today a picture which in many ways is similar to what we see among the North American or Mexican Indians, namely a thin veneer of Christian religion, but there is one difference namely that with the Indians the veneer is about something, namely their old Pagan tradition, and with us, I am afraid it is about nothing. It is just a veneer, and there is not an old, strong, and potentially religious tradition which is underneath.

Because of this vacuum new religions have developed, which have taken the place of the older religions, the new religions being essentially the *religion of fascism* and the *religion of Stalinism*, which are religions in the sense in which I define religion, namely a frame of reference, and an object of devotion. Since it is not the question of religion or not, but only good or bad religion, it is no qualification in any value sense to call fascism and Stalinism a religion. It is only a statement about a system which gives a frame of reference, and which gives an object of devotion, for which people are not only willing to die, which is bad enough, but are also willing to give up their reason, which is perhaps worse, and yet this is what this type of religion can produce. They could arise, they could assume this tremendous power and appeal, because of the religious vacuum which is growing stronger and stronger in the twentieth century and which was less strong in the nineteenth century, when at least the moral tradition of religion was a more potent factor in the life of people than it is today.

In the United States, you find peculiar things which are substitutes for religion in small ways. If you think, for instance, of a movement like the Scientology Church which is centered around a book called *Dianetics*, written by L. Ron Hubbard (1950). This perfectly crazy book becomes the center of attention, worship, not only of stupid people, but of some of the most intelligent intellectuals. It is an amazing phenomenon, and yet apparently the need for something, to have faith in, even if it is, or because it is absurd, because it transcends common sense, because it constitutes some irrational hope in something, is enough to become the center of attention and interest of thousands and thousands of people.—I am sure there are many other small movements in the United States today, which have the same function. You can say that in a certain sense, the fad for psychoanalysis, while it is certainly not as irrational as *Dianetics*, also has some earmarks and some qualities of the searching for a new religion in which one can simply believe. And Freud, with his dogmatism, made it kind of easy to do that.

I believe one point has a great deal to do with our religious vacuum, and that is the problem of the absence of the dramatic element, of the *absence of ritual in our modern culture.* Life in general moves between two poles, the pole of routine, and the pole of the dramatic, the heightened dramatic experience which breaks through the routine. I assume that routine plays a great role and must play a great role because it guarantees in a way, that we eat and drink and work. If there were not a good deal of routine in our life, everything would explode. We would perhaps feel, like in Heaven, because of the intensity of our feelings of inner experience. However, everything would go to pieces, and no organized society could exist.

There is a good deal of necessity for routine, for being concerned with the hum-drum in life, with that which is really not important, and yet which is very important from the standpoint of our survival as individuals and as groups. But at the same time, routine has the great danger for man because with this routine, which in itself is rooted in one aspect of ourselves, namely our animal aspect, in the need to eat and drink, this same routine tends to cover up, to paralyze and eventually to kill that which is our spiritual side, that which is the most important thing in life, namely, if you don't mind my saying so, our soul, our experience of love, of thought, of beauty. There is in every individual life, and in every culture you might say, a struggle and conflict between that part of life and that part of a culture which is routine, and that part which touches upon the basic human experience.

Most cultures do something about the latter thing, and they do it most effectively in the form of the dramatic. I use the word dramatic here because I refer to the Greek drama. The Greek drama was not at all what your drama is today, something for which you buy a ticket, and you go there as a consumer, and you find it good if the *New York Times* has written about it that it is good, and you are satisfied. But the Greek drama was a ritual. It was a religious ritual, in which the basic experiences of every human being were presented in a dramatic form, and this dramatic form was capable of smashing through the routine. The individual who participated in this drama was not a consumer. He was not an onlooker, but he was participating in a ritual which touched in him, that which is the most important thing in life and the drama had, as they say, a cathartic effect. It cleansed something. It touched something. While participating in the dramatic performance, the person was brought in touch again with the deepest human thing in him and in humanity. In participating in the drama, he was capable again and again of smashing through that layer in him which is the routine.

The same you have in the Catholic religion. The ritual of the Catholic religion is dramatic. I am not speaking about the particular contents now, but the formal element in life, and in society, that in the participation in the ritual, you also got in touch with some of the fundamental aspects of yourself, and because of the dramatic formulation of resurrection, of birth, of death, of God, of the Virgin, or whatever it is, because of the beauty of the garments, because of the beauty of the churches, the participant was capable of experiencing something so profound, and something which, like the Greek drama, penetrated the layers of routine and inner laziness.

Let me give you an example of my recent experience: a bull-fight. The bull-fight, as it is practiced in Spanish countries, in Middle America, is not a sport, just as little as the Greek drama was like our modern dramas or our plays are. The bull-fight is a ritual with a very specific content, namely symbolizing the fight between brute matter and spirit, intelligence and gracefulness. These two principles are fighting with each other, symbolized by the bull, and the bull-fighter. It ends usually with the defeat and death of the bull, and what you witness in this ritual is the very vivid experience of the death of pure matter, and the victory of man. It is a ritual which brings us close to some of the most fundamental experiences, and I think for most American visitors, too close. Usually they feel that it is cruel. I don't think that is the real reason. They are just not accustomed to be brought so close to the facts of life and the facts of death, but all this is camouflaged aid concealed.

Where in our culture is a place for the function of the dramatic, for the function of the ritual? Where does our culture provide for this experience, which really most great cultures do provide for? The only ritual which we really have, is the ritual of competition between two men, or between two groups of men, and that is the ritual meaning of our interest in baseball, football, and in a Presidential election. There is a real problem. There are some of the basic facts of life, two men fighting. But really, it can by no means be compared to the depth of the problem which you find even in the bull-fight, because it is really one of the simple, crude problems of life, that two men are fighting, and one is going to win. So what? This is a situation which has a certain relevance, but really, compared with the great problems of human existence, and life as expressed in the rituals of all great cultures, it is an awfully secondary problem. But that is about all we have.

There seems to be a need for more. The Nazis and Stalinists sense that. They introduce new rituals. Undoubtedly, the success of these systems was partly based on the fact that they were capable of satisfying the human sense for the dramatic. With us, in our culture, how can people satisfy it?

If you have an automobile accident, you will see that twenty, thirty people stand around to look. Why? It doesn't make any sense, but I think it makes a lot of sense, because that is almost the only chance to get in touch with death, with something dramatic. It is the lowest form of the dramatic which exists, but at least it is there. I know of a case, I don't remember where it was, where a woman was murdered in a house. Two weeks later there were hundreds of people driving out with their cars to the suburbs somewhere to look at that house. Well, that makes just as little sense as these people who watched the automobile accident. They don't want to help, but they are not so dumb either. There is a little bit, in the most trivial form, which nevertheless gets one in touch with that which, in the dramatic, in the ritual of a more developed culture, in this sense is expressed in a way which has a cathartic effect.

Obviously, to look at a fire, to look at an automobile accident, to look at a murder scene, has no cathartic effect, but still the impulse is very strong, because that is about the last remnant of getting in touch with anything dramatic in a culture which has almost completely cultivated the routine, and not the dramatic. I have even a suspicion that the function of detective stories, while I like to read them very much, nevertheless is one of the things in which we get in touch with a little bit of the dramatic. There are at least a few people murdered. It is kind of dramatic, the question of will the sinner be found out, or will he not be found out. Will justice catch up with him or not. You have, in a very clever, and as I think, amusing form, a little bit of the metaphysical problem.

We are starved for any touch with the realities of life because our realities are artifacts. They are the realities of conventions and cars, but we are starved for any touch with that which, in most cultures, was provided for by religion or by the equivalent of religion, and with us, there is hardly anything which is worth while to mention.

I want to proceed now by discussing at first some of the main concepts which I think ought to be understood a little bit more clearly, in order to evaluate the state of mind in contemporary society, and I shall come after this, to the discussion of the crucial issues, at least as I see them, of mental health for our culture.

## b) About the concept of work

Let me begin by talking about the concept of work, and let me try to sketch, very briefly, certain developments which I believe are important to understand. You might begin with a statement that work is the great liberator of man, that man begins his history, his real human history, when he begins to work. At the moment when he begins to work, he merges from the primitive unity with nature, and in the process of distancing himself from nature, in the process of becoming the one who changes nature, he changes himself. He becomes a creator, rather than to be part of nature. Man develops faculties of reason, of art. He develops the capacity to express his powers in relation to nature, and he develops himself as an individual in this process.

Undoubtedly, human development is based on work, and is to a large extent, accompanied by the development of the faculties of man. In this sense, we can speak of work as the liberator of man, as the most important factor in the development of man. We may add therefore, that the way in which man does work, is one of the most important factors in the development of his whole personality. You might say that in medieval society this function of work as a liberating, emancipating, developing force found one of its highest developments. I don't mean just in the Middle Ages. There are many other periods of human history where something like that occurred.

There you found that the artisan had become a productive, original individual and enjoyed the process of work, doing things which are beautiful. Up to this day, we find this rather difficult to repeat, and that holds true not only for the Middle Ages, but holds true for many cultures in the world, even some of which we call "primitive." But then a very curious development occurs with the beginning of the modern period, specifically in the Protestant, northern countries. The pleasure in work changed into a duty. To work became something abstract, a duty, a means to an end and originally in Calvinist and Protestant thinking, it became a means of salvation. It became a religious act, but it became abstract in this process. It was not any more essentially the pleasure in creating a beautiful chair, or jewelry or something, but it was a sign that if one was successful, it meant that one had God's grace, that one was among the chosen ones. You might say that work as fulfillment, as pleasure, changed into work as obsession, as duty, and as something which was in itself painful, as any obsessional activity is, but nevertheless which had a very important function, to keep men in a mental balance, because there was nothing he really felt secure in but this type of work.

This function of work is correctly described only for the middle class, for the entrepreneur, for the man who had a truck or a factory, but it does not hold true specifically in the eighteenth and nineteenth century for the man who had to sell his labor, who had not any meaningful work in the sense of individual initiative. The laborer who worked fourteen or sixteen hours a day in the eighteenth or nineteenth century, and the child who worked ten hours in a factory, they were not compulsively driven to work. They did not have the moral benefits of believing—they served their Lord by working like mad. Theirs was forced work, necessitated by the need to avoid starvation, and nothing but that essentially.

With the beginning of the modern age you have two branches of the concept and the reality of work: compulsive work which had a certain religious meaning in the Protestant Calvinist frame of reference, and of course, you might say forced labor, which was that work to which the poorer classes were forced. That was the only way they wouldn't starve, and economic conditions were such that the economic pressure grew rather than to become less, in the course of the nineteenth century.

In the twentieth century you have a new development, because work had lost a great deal of the Protestant Calvinist quality of duty, which it had in the nineteenth century. We are not so obsessed any more, as our grandparents were, with that compulsion to work, but there is something new. We work in a very special sense for the growth of the idol machine. The machine which is worshipped is a machine which works, and we are fascinated today by something which is different from the medieval concept of work, from the Protestant concept of work, which is even not any more the nineteenth century concept of profit which is so important. But we are fascinated today by the growth of a productive machine. Production per se is one of the great fantasies we are worshipping. It has become an aim in life, to see how things grow, not organic things, not flowers, but greater and bigger machines, more good produced, faster cars.

This is one line of the development of work: work as a meaningful fulfillment of human purposes, work as compulsion and duty, work essentially for profit, and work you might say, as an act of worship to the altar of the machine, which has a value and a meaning in itself.

How has the other line—in regard to the *worker*—developed? For the worker at the beginning of the nineteenth century, work was slavery. Work was forced labor, but we have seen a tremendous development, in which the situation of the working class has changed fundamentally, and today we have an eight hour day, or even less. Work has lost completely this role of forced labor, of something creating great hardship, but of course one thing has not changed. Work has not become pleasurable, meaningful, for the worker, although in recent years, there are many studies and attempts at least to find out whether industrial work could not be more meaningful. I shall come back to this later.

The social structure of a country like the United States, has changed tremendously, namely that the number of people who are employed, who are working in one sense or another, who get wages and salaries, is increasing tremendously. We find today as one of the great longings among people, a vision of complete laziness, an ideal that one day I won't have to work at all. Take the advertising of the Life Insurance Companies, of that mysterious couple who travel around on two hundred dollars a month, and all they feel is they don't have to work any more. The most attractive vision in life is the vision that one day I won't have to do anything. Therefore students before the age of twenty-five, before they take a job in a big company, inquire as to what their retirement plans are. This is very characteristic for our age.

Take these little things, which are very important and suggestive. During World War II there was a series of advertisements for an ice-box which you can push a button and it turns around so you have saved the tremendous trouble of reaching in there to get something out, and I am sure there were hundreds of thousands of people who were looking for the happiness focused on that wonderful ice-box which they might buy, which saves them that work.

Take even our cars, where you don't have to shift a gear. Well, that may be very practical, and I can see, from a safety standpoint, they say it is so advantageous, which I can't judge, but—I think the appeal is not at all the safety fact. The appeal is because it's a vision of effortless power, of having push-button power, of being able to move something without making any effort. That is, to a large extent, the attitude behind television. I am not speaking against television now, but I mean to say that I am sure that among the psychological motivations why this fascinates people, why people are just starry-eyed at this wonderful machine, is that there they sit in this chair, push a button, and the whole world appears. The President appears, or world events appear, and if one can catch a fire, or a tragedy somewhere, it would appear too, and all they do is to sit and to move that button.—If you think about it, and go over our advertising for all sorts of products, you find again the tremendous appeal of that complete laziness, in which you don't have to make any effort, and yet in which you have great power.

The other day I was watching an acquaintance of mine who had his little three-year-old boy push the starter button of his car. I was so shocked that I didn't say anything, but imagine what that means to a three year old boy. Although he doesn't know anything about it, he can hardly move a little wooden car of ten, twenty pounds, there he is, already having the experience that with a little bit of energy, he can start a one-hundred-twenty horsepower machine. That is the way we feel and think. Paradoxically as it sounds, that our ability to produce a bomb which might destroy the whole universe, and which is released by some man in the air pushing a button, is in a certain sense, part of that whole fantasy, that even the most destructive power is something which can be employed by just moving your finger half-an-inch.

## c) The worship of production and consumption

One form of our contemporary religion is the worship of a specific idol—the idol of *production per se*. The problem one hundred years ago was more the problem that we did not produce for use, but for profit, that the profit motive was the essential one. Today the problem is not any more so much production for profit, but production for nothing, the production of everything, because production in itself has become a God, has become an end in itself, and people are simply fascinated by the act of production, as in religious cultures they would be fascinated by religious symbols.

We all living in that culture, don't see that being fascinated by the act of production is a religious attitude. We find it quite natural, because it is not phrased in religious terms, because when we speak of religion we speak about Christianity or Judaism, we speak about the cross, or religious ritual. Therefore, in our conscious minds, we don't call it religion when we are so fascinated by serving this machinery of production. If you take modern man, this is one part of the frame of reference in which he lives, and one of the religious objects of devotion to which he devotes his life, that things are bigger and better, that there is more and more.

Quite parallel to that, is the problem of consumption. Obviously we consume in order to have pleasure. We eat something because it tastes good, or we have a house because it is nice, and we want to live in it. There is a very realistic point in consumption, namely to serve our needs, and to serve our pleasures. But it seems to me, just as production has become an aim in itself, *consumption has become an aim in itself*. We are fascinated by the idea of buying things, without much reference to how useful they are. This is one of the psychological factors on which our economy is based. It is furthered and stimulated by the advertising people, who make a business out of applying this knowledge to the practical question, how to sell their product to consumers.

We find today very little pleasure in anything people buy. The idea is you get something new as quick as possible and actually if I would imagine the Heaven of a modern city, how contemporary man would imagine it, it is not any more the Heaven of the Mohammedans or anything like that, but it is a Heaven which consists of gadgets for which you have all the money to buy ice-boxes, television and all the newest gadgets which are on the market. There is no limitation to your buying power, and you can buy a new model every year. Probably you can buy in Heaven a new model every day, because that is Heaven. The process of thought in this fantasy of Paradise is the faster production of gadgets. You have that which you never have quite in real life. You can really buy everything. You have not this thing dangling in front of your nose every day, hoping that next year, two years from now, you can buy it, but it is there.

I really don't think I am making fun but this is really what goes on, except that we don't experience that in terms of our religious vision of Paradise, because that is reserved for the more explicit forms of religion. This attitude of buying, this religious expectation that there are endless things which we can get, and the almost orgastic pleasure in visualizing the wealth of new things you can buy, this is something which carries over in our attitude towards things other than new models. We have become consumers of everything, consumers of science, consumers of art, consumers of lectures, consumers of love, and the attitude is always the same. I pay and I get something, and I am entitled to get it. I do not have to make any spatial great effort, because it is always the same problem of exchange of things which I buy and things which I get. This same attitude of the consumer in a sense, you find in many parallel phenomena, in people's experience toward art, toward science, towards love, as what they experience when they buy the latest model. In fact, that is the way one gets married. It has a great deal to do with the latest model as we see it, which is the most successful one. The one which to attain seems to be very appealing, and a proof of one's value.

Instead of the traditional concept of work as pleasure, or work as duty, two features of our contemporary religion, as far as it exists, are the worship of production and the worship of consumption, both not related to any reality which makes sense in terms of human existence.

I imagine that if tomorrow we had a state of affairs in which people would have to work four hours a day, and they would get twice or three times the wages, this is something which Norman Thomas, or the representatives of the "New Deal" [the economic and social politics under President F. D. Roosevelt], and I think many members of the Republic Party, would also describe as a very desirable goal. In fact, it would correspond to the keenest dreams of the socialist fifty years ago. That is much more drastic and radical than what Karl Marx wrote is the immediate goal of socialism or of revolution. I imagine that such a thing could be. What would happen? What a catastrophe that would be! How many nervous breakdowns and psychoses you would have, because people would absolutely not know what to do with their lives, their time. They would be crazy buying things. They would change their cars every half-year. They would even then experience a profound disappointment that this Heaven, the attainment of all this, just doesn't make sense, that it is meaningless.

What keeps this really going is only the fact that you never reach that Heaven. It remains always far away. Therefore, you have the comfort that one day, there really would be a solution and salvation, but since you rarely experience that day, according to the statistics of income of the majority, you always have this hope which is never quite disappointed, because you always think it is not enough yet, and if it were more, then you would be happy. But if any such state of affairs would occur, in which people would only have to work two or three or four hours, and would have many times their income, this would be a real catastrophe.

For thousands of years writers and Utopians in the most moving words have described that the most beautiful aim of life is a life in which one spends only a little time working for the necessities to keep alive, in which there is a wealth of commodities and no need, imagine what it means that quite realistically, if this life could be achieved for today, one would have to make every effort to avoid it, because it would lead to a real psychic disaster. We are not prepared at all to make sense of our lives and of our time, but that is part of the picture of this religion of production and consumption in which both have become unrelated to the real and concrete human needs of anyone.

## d) About happiness and security

Let me now speak about some other concepts which we use, and which we ought to clarify. We are still very much concerned with the concept of *happiness*. That is an old tradition, and we still use this word, and we say our aim is to be happy. Two or three hundred years ago, in the Protestant countries, this was not the aim. The aim was pleasing God, living up to our conscience, but today we say we want to be happy, and what do we mean by being happy? Well, I guess if you ask people honestly, most will say if they are not too sophisticated, that it is having fun. What is having fun? You all know what people consider to have fun, and indeed it has very little to do with what in other cultures has been described as happiness. People don't even try to visualize that happiness. Is that a state of mind, or is one perhaps happy in a few rare moments of one's life? Is it a rare fruit of a tree which blossoms only rarely, but which has to be there in order to bear this fruit once in a while?

I should like to say one word about happiness from a psychological standpoint. You will find that many people would define happiness as the opposite of sadness or suffering. Suffering and sadness is one thing, and happiness is its opposite. From that standpoint they have a vision of or concept of happiness as one in which I have no pain, no disturbance, and no sadness. There is something fundamentally wrong with that concept, because if you do not experience sadness, you are not alive, and if you are not alive, you can not be happy. Life is something in which sadness and pain are as essential a part of being alive as happiness. So happiness is certainly not the opposite of something else which clinically speaking you can observe very accurately, the opposite of depression.

What is depression? Depression is not sadness. A person who is really depressed would thank God for being able to be sad. Depression is the inability to feel. Depression is a sense of being dead while your body is alive. Depression is not at all the same, not even related to pain and sadness. It is an inability of experiencing joy, as well as of experiencing sadness. It is a lack of any feeling. It is a sense of deadness, which is unbearable for the person who is depressed. That is why it is so altogether unbearable, the very fact of not being able to feel.

Happiness is one of the forms in which intense living is expressed. The experience of intense living, according to Spinoza's definition, is identical with joy or with happiness, and on the other pole, you have depression which is essentially the absence of feeling. In intense living, you have pain as well as joy, and they belong together because they are both outcomes of the intensity of living. As the opposite of both, you have depression, lack of intensity of feeling. If you tell an average person today that one of, if not the most painful mental sickness which exists, is absence of feeling, I think there will be many people who will just not understand it. In fact, there are many people who will say: "But that is wonderful. That is perfect, if I don't feel anything. What the hell should I feel? I want to be quiet. I want not to have trouble." They don't know the almost unbearable experience of a very different kind of state of mind in which one can not feel anything.

In the sense of this definition, the normal person in our culture is considerably depressed, because his intensity of feeling is considerably reduced. People who get a depression these days, are just perhaps not more un-alive and alienated from themselves and out of touch with reality than the rest of us, but we have defenses against it and they don't. There are plenty of defenses against the feeling which comes from not being alive. Our amusement industry, work, our cocktail parties, our chatter, the whole routine which we have, are all so many defenses against that terrible moment when we really feel that we don't feel anything. That protects us from getting melancholia. There are a few individuals who are not protected, maybe because their sensitivity is greater. Maybe this state of mind where they don't feel, to them is felt in a more sensitive fashion, and therefore the defenses don't work so well.

We find as a general state of mind—although of course only in a statistical sense and not valid for everybody—a general reduction of intensity of feeling close to depression, however mitigated and in fact compensated for by the many defenses which we call pleasure and work.

We use another term very much which has become even a slogan in many political discussions: the word *security*. You find many psychiatrists today and psychoanalysts and so on, who say the aim of life is to be secure, to feel secure. Parents get rather frightened and when they bring up their children they are terribly worried whether the children feel secure. If the child sees another child who has more than he has, it has to be bought right away because he will feel secure. Security is essentially defined in terms of living up to the market standards of personality. Allegedly, some psychiatrists have formulated that one feels secure if one is successful, accomplished, up to standards, to represent a pattern that is successful. We are obsessed by security as an aim of life.

Some critics are convinced that the interest of people to be secure undermines the spirit of initiative. But then they are talking about certain elementary economic securities, of old-age pensions and so on, when they don't question the fact that a man whose aim is to save a million dollars in order to be secure in his old age, or buys life insurance, that is not under the condemnable attitude of security. Nevertheless, they have a point there, namely that our life is geared around a sense of psychic security, in which life loses all sense of adventure. Men like Mussolini, for instance, who was a great coward, but who had a sense for the dramatic, coined the slogan that one should live dangerously. Well, he didn't, although his end was rather bad in spite of all the precautions he took to the contrary. But he sensed that people had a sense for life as an adventure.

The aim of psychic development is to be able to tolerate insecurity, because if one has any sense on this planet, we are in every way insecure, not because of the atom bomb, but because of the whole way we exist. We are insecure physically, we are insecure mentally and spiritually. We know almost nothing compared with what we ought to know. We try to live in a sensible way with almost no information about how to do it. We risk not so much our physical life, but our spiritual life, almost every minute. We have mostly misinformation about the process of living, and if we think about it, we are indeed terribly insecure. Any person who becomes aware even for a moment, of the fundamental, essential aloneness of himself as an individual, must feel insecure. And in fact, he can't afford this experience even for a minute if he is not related to the world, in which he can have the courage to relate himself—or to use Dr. Tillich's words, *The Courage to Be* (P. Tillich, 1952).

We tend to create people who have no courage, who don't dare to live in an exciting or intense fashion, who are trained to seek as a goal in life, security, which in this way, can only be brought about by complete conforming, and by complete deadness. In this sense you might say joy and security are complete contradictory, because joy is a result of the intensity of living. If you live intensely, you must be able to bear a great deal of insecurity, because then life is a terribly risky business at every moment. You can only hope that you don't falter, and that you don't completely take the wrong road in this process.

Of course people have still a sense of adventure. This sense of being so secure and losing all sense of adventure in life is so terribly boring that it becomes quite impossible. Therefore various types of movies, of books, and again perhaps detective stories take care of that. Or vicariously, you read about people who get a divorce every year, and even that is then felt as something which is at least an adventure, although it is by no means as brave as it sounds.

# 3. ALIENATION AND THE PROBLEM OF MENTAL HEALTH

# (THIRD LECTURE: FEBRUARY 2, 1953)

## a) Alienation and abstractification

I should like to speak about what seems to me to be the central problem of mental health: self alienation, i.e. the alienation from ourselves, from our own feelings, from people and from nature, or to put it still differently, the alienation between ourselves, and the world inside and outside of ourselves.

Let me try to explain what is meant by the word "alienation." Literally speaking of course, it means that we are aliens to ourselves, or the world outside is alien to us. Since that are still just words I have to explain a little more what I mean.

One essential feature in modern society and in our present economy is the role of the market. You may ask what the market has to do with the question of psychology. I believe that to a large extent people in every society are formed by the economic and social conditions under which they live. This was one of the great discoveries of Karl Marx, and while he may have dogmatically exaggerated and overstated his theory, as I think he did, while he did in my opinion underestimate many human factors, many factors belonging not to the realm of the economic, I still do believe that this was one of the most far-reaching, most fundamental approaches to the understanding of society. It is very foolish to permit the Stalinists to claim that they are using the Marxist theory when their claim is about as valid as that of the Catholic inquisition to speak in the name of Christ. I think it is foolish not only because it is not true, but because it leads to ignoring one of the greatest forces in sociology. (There is still another reason: If one happens to be of the belief, as I am myself, that the Stalinist system is one of the most inhuman and cruel systems which ever existed in the world, by aiding their claim that they are the true successors of Marx, we simply are aiding them and not at all doing the opposite, namely providing a clarification of this concept. I am saying this because living in Mexico for two-and-a-half years, I get the impression that the word Marxism is a word that is used like a hot potato, and I don't think that this is any help to American democracy and to scientific thinking.)

I am speaking about an economy which is centered around the market. Most comparatively primitive system uses markets. You have a market like in small villages many generations ago, like you still have in Mexico and less developed countries, in which people come to the market and sell their goods to customers who come from places around. They know pretty much who will come. They enjoy very much seeing the people and talking to them. It is not only a business place, but a place of pleasure and entertainment. If you take this more primitive form of a market, you find that there something very concrete happens: Things are brought to the market which are produced for a certain purpose. One knows more or less the people who will come and buy. The whole thing is a very concrete situation of exchange.

Our modern economy is governed by the market in an entirely different sense. It is not governed by a market where people sit and sell their wares, but what you might call a National Commodity, in which prices are determined and production is determined by demand. This "national market" is the regulating factor for modern economy. Your prices are not determined by any economic group who says that and that must be paid. This is something exceptional in wartime or in certain situations. Your price or while existence is determined by the operation of the market, which constantly tends to equalize and to balance itself up to a certain point.

What is the meaning of all this in psychological terms? What happens on the market is that all things appear as commodities. What is the difference between a thing and a commodity? This glass of water here is a thing which at the moment I can use to hold water and so on. It is very useful to me. It is not particularly pretty, but it is what it is. However, as a commodity it is something I can buy, which has a certain price, and I perceive of it not only as this thing, as something which has a certain *use value* as they say, but as a commodity which has a certain *exchange value*. It appears as a commodity in the market, and its function as a commodity is that I can describe it as a fifty-cent or twenty-five cent thing. I can express this thing in terms of money, or in terms of an abstraction.

This leads us to a step further. Take, for instance, something very simple which is rather paradoxical. You can say the value of one Rembrandt painting is five times the value of a Cadillac. That is a perfectly sensible statement, because you compare the Rembrandt painting and the Cadillac in terms of an abstraction, namely you can express them in terms of money. Actually it is a very absurd statement because a Rembrandt painting, concretely speaking, has nothing to do whatsoever with a Cadillac. There is one way of comparing, of making a sentence in which the two are brought into any kind of relationship, by putting each into the abstract form of money. Thus you are able to compare the two in the sense of a particular relationship, in which one can say the value of one thing is five times the value of another thing. And indeed, if you take your own attitude toward things, if you analyze it a little, you will find that you relate yourself to things to a large extent, not as concrete things, but as commodities. You perceive already of a thing in terms of its abstract money value, in terms of its exchange value. You think of this glass, for instance, not simply as a not very beautiful but useful thing, but as of a cheap thing, a twenty-five cent or fifty-cent thing.

Take for instance a newspaper report or anything like that which says: "The five-million-dollar bridge was finished," "the ten-million-dollar hotel was built." Here you have already the concept of the thing not in terms of its use value, not in terms of its beauty that is there, not in terms of any other concrete thing which is present in this, but in terms of the abstract meaning, that this is worth so much in terms of its exchange value, and therefore can be compared with anything else, provided we relate ourselves to that abstraction, its exchange value.

Now what does this mean? In our system a process happens for which I should like to coin a word, provided it doesn't already exist, namely the *process of abstractification*. Forgive me this coinage, but I find it useful. By abstractification I mean to make something abstract rather than to leave it as it is concretely. We are accustomed, by the way we produce, by the way our economy functions, to experience in the first place, things in their abstract forms, rather than their concrete forms. We relate ourselves to them in terms of the exchange value, rather than in terms of their use value.

Let me give you a few examples how far this goes. The *New York Times* wrote a few days ago: "Bachelor of Science plus Ph.D. equals $40,000." I was puzzled, and then I read that it meant that if a student gets a Ph. D., then the average earning in a lifetime will be $40,000 more than if he has only the Bachelor of Science. The *New York Times* is a very serious paper, and certainly in its headlines never makes fun of anything. I think this is just at random, a very characteristic way in which people feel things today, that the Bachelor of Science, the Ph.D. become commodities which can be measured, and really put into a formula of an equation. The other item which I read in *Newsweek* was that the Eisenhower government feels that it has such a capital of confidence, that in a few weeks or more they can undertake some unpopular measures, because their capital of confidence is so great, that they can afford to lose some of it.—That is perfectly alright with me, but what I am referring to, is not the political issue, but the way of thinking.

One thinks of confidence as a capital which one can afford to lose, provided there is much of it, and again it is the same thing as "A Bachelor of Science plus a Ph.D. equals $40,000." The problem of confidence, of a relationship between a party or government to the people, is expressed in the abstract formula of something which is measurable, which can be quantified, which is not any more something concrete, but which is something abstract, which can be related in a quantitative fashion to everything else in this world. It is a process of abstractification in which all specific, concrete qualities get more or less lost, and everything assumes the same quantifiable quality of being expressed in the abstract form of money, or any other form of abstraction, which I shall talk about presently.

Take for instance another example. What is the greatest distance in the world today? Well that would be about more or less between New York and Bombay, India. I don't know how many miles that is really, but I do know it is about three-and-a-half days, and I think it is about $800 or $1,000 worth of distance, and in fact, this is the most realistic way in which you can express distance, the differences between the time you need to travel. Even the greatest distance is so greatly reduced in time because there are no two places which are further apart than about three-and-a-half days. Then really, the only real problem you have is how much worth the distance is in terms of money, and $1,000 is the largest distance. Of course, if you want to get back, it is a $ 2,000 distance.—What I mean to say is, this is another way, another area, in which we think in abstract terms, in which we can even express time and space in terms of money, and in fact, this is not so nonsensical. It is useful in a sense, but it is another example of the lack of concreteness in our experience, and of our tendency to experience things abstracted from their concrete qualities.

## b) Alienated experience

The same obviously holds true for our experience of ourselves and of others. You read, for instance, an item in the *New York Times*, let us say, an obituary, which says, "Shoe manufacturer dies. Railroad engineer dies." Who died? A shoe manufacturer. A man died or a woman died, but if you describe even death in terms of the subject being "shoe manufacturer," what you do, for example, is the same as if you say this is a fifty-cent thing. You forget and ignore the concreteness of that person, who was a very specific, concrete person, and like every person, somebody quite unique. You ignore all the concrete qualities, and you abstractify.

You speak of him as of "the shoe manufacturer," as if that had been he. That is so to speak the equivalent of speaking of a commodity in terms of its exchange value, in terms of its price.

It would make more sense, of course, if you would report on a convention of shoe manufacturers in Atlantic City, and would then refer to Mr. Jones as a shoe manufacturer, because at least this would be a concrete explanation of what he is doing there. He is there to discuss the business of manufacturing shoes. But can you imagine, you speak of the death of a person, which aside from birth, is one of the most fundamental events in our existence, in the existence of anybody, and then you refer to the subject of this event as "a shoe manufacturer?" Then indeed, you have a picture of an almost complete abstractification of concrete things, namely of people.

There is a whole other realm which is connected with this, in which people become abstractified (which I have discussed in a chapter in *Man for Himself* under the title, "The Marketing Orientation"). People do not only sell their physical power, their skill, their brain, being hired for one or the other purpose, but in our culture they sell also their personalities, that is to say, they have to be pleasant, they have to have the right background, if possible, they have to have kids in order to make them respectable. Even the wife has to be pleasant and has to fit, generally speaking a certain pattern. The man has to be nice, and all the nicer the farther you want to get the individual does not feel himself as this concrete individual who eats, and drinks and sleeps and loves and hates, who is somebody unique and somebody concrete, but as a commodity, as something which has—and I say intentionally which *has*—to sell itself on the market successfully. He must cultivate the qualities which are in demand and if he feels he is in demand he is successful, and he feels himself a failure if he is not in demand.

The whole sense of value of an individual—if one will call it an individual—depends on whether he is saleable or not, whether there is a demand for him or not. For this reason his of self, his sense of inner confidence never depends on the appreciation of his real concrete qualities, intelligence, honesty, integrity, his humor, anything he is, but on whether or not he succeeds in selling himself. Therefore, of course, he is always insecure, always dependent on success, and gets frantically insecure if this success is not forthcoming.

## c) Alienated language

Language is another form in which this process of abstractification goes on. Language has a purpose, a function, which is to be able to convey, to communicate, and therefore naturally language has to abstractify. If I speak of this watch, and if I call it a watch, I mean by that not this particular concrete watch. While this watch is not unique, it is nevertheless only one of many thousands of watches made by the same firm, but it does not cover other watches. When I say that is a watch, I say this is something which has enough in common with all other watches that we can understand each other by referring to an abstraction, a watch, rather than to something entirely concrete, which is this particular one. That is the function of language, to abstractify, to abstract from the concrete unique phenomena, which permits me to cover numerous objects of similar kinds with one word, provided there is room for this abstraction.

But abstractions also present a danger, namely the danger that in speaking about things in a word, they lose their concreteness and that I do not experience any more that which I am talking about. I experience only a word. "A rose is a rose is a rose. . . ." That is the protest against this process of abstraction, because in this line the rose is made a very concrete experience. Ask yourself what goes on if you say a rose. Do you see the rose? Do you smell it? Do you feel it as something concrete, or perhaps when you say a rose you think of five dollars a dozen, or you have a vague concept of an elegant flower which you may send at the proper occasion. How concretely do we experience something we denote with a word? Or do we use language essentially in terms of abstraction?

Certainly, if the owner of a flower shop, making his balance in the evening, and writing down he sold fifty roses, would get wrapped up in enthusiasm when he thinks about these roses, he probably would forget to count correctly. He would just sit there with a wonderful feeling of smelling, and fantasy of seeing these roses before his eyes. He would leave his shop happily, but he would forget to make his balance, and he couldn't conduct his business. But what I am saying is not just a joke.—This process of abstraction is a very important part of our existence, our modern existence, which is based very essentially on a rational system of bookkeeping, of making a balance, of quantifying things. Our system could not exist without our elaborate methods in which we are capable of quantifying things in business. We are capable of quantifying labor costs, entertainment costs, and even the money we spend for what is called human relations. All this is quantifiable, and certainly I am far from criticizing this in itself, because it is part and parcel of our modern way of producing and our great business and productive entity couldn't possibly exist, our whole economic system would collapse if we did not have the means and the attitude to quantify business processes.

The question however is, whether this mode of production, this mode of behaving economically hasn't had a tremendous influence on all our personalities, and has not transcended by far the shop and the business, and has gone into our whole life, so that the man who owns the flower shop not only doesn't think of a concrete flower, but of a fifty-cent thing when he makes a balance, but he never thinks of a concrete flower. He might sell cheese tomorrow or atomic energy or shoes the next day. All these things have very little concrete meaning, but they are essentially experienced as things which have this abstract value.

This becomes even much more important if we consider those words which do not refer to things, but to inner experiences, so we speak of love. What do we mean? It is utterly fantastic that there is nothing under the sun almost which is not called love. Cruelty and dependence and domination and real love and fear and conventionality, almost everything is called love. I love him may express anything from slight sympathy, or just a polite expression of not hating a person, to those feelings which the great poets have talked about or written poems about. It is all the same word.

I was listening to a psychiatrist the other day talking about a patient, and he said about him that he had a significant job, and I asked him, what do you mean by significant, and he said, "Well, it is a rather important job in the business hierarchy." All right, what is significant about it? If you want to say he is highly paid and it is a prestigeful job, all right. But why call it significant? Then he went on to explain further and I tried to see why this was all significant, in what sense. As far as I could understand, there was no significance whatsoever, except that it was highly paid, and had a certain amount of prestige, and if I said that Professor Einstein would be busy with significant things, I think it would be an understatement, but it refers to something concrete.

That is our language in general. "I am tickled to death."

What for? What about? It is a complete embarrassment in this expression, an expression of one doesn't feel anything. One isn't capable of expressing anything. Strangely enough, death plays a great role in these expressions. I am dying to do this or that, to express some intense excitement about something, and I am afraid the usage of the word death or dying is not entirely accidental, but is an expression that all these words come out of a deep emptiness and out of a lack of feeling, and out of that sense of depression which I was talking about last time when I was discussing the concept of happiness.

We use language today not any more only for purposes of communication, but to a large extent in the sense that words have almost become the same as money, abstractions of real experiences which are interchanged in human communication without being experienced as referring to concrete experiences. You ask a man who is deeply unhappy how he is and he says: "I am fine." You may say there is a certain pride in that, but I think the main point is that no one expects that the other person is really interested, and that words don't count. You use words to fill in the gaps, the vacuum in yourself and in the communication between you and another person. Listen to the tone of voice in which human communication goes on. How abstract all this is. It is almost like going to the market, buying things. Here are two dollars and I get the thing I ask for.

People exchange words without sharing any reality which they are talking about. They are exchanging words in a certain embarrassment, to cover up the emptiness which exists in their communication, and they don't feel stimulated. After the talk, they don't feel they have shared something. They have a kind of empty feeling which you have whenever you have been for two hours in a movie which turns out to be very poor, and you leave with a certain feeling of embarrassment and shame at having spent that time with such nonsense.

## d) Alienated feelings and sentimentality

So far I wanted to give a description of what seems to me one of the essential features and dangers in man in contemporary society, namely that *we have become out of touch with all realities* except one, that is the man-made reality of business, of organization of things we can manipulate. We are in contact with artifacts. We are in contact with social routine, and we are in contact and refer to that which produces more things, but we are not in contact with the basic realities of human existence. We are not in contact with our feelings, with what is really our feeling, with our happiness, unhappiness, our fear and doubt, and all the things that go on in a human being. We are not in contact with our fellow man or nature. We are only in contact with a small segment of the world created by ourselves, and actually we are deeply afraid of touching anything deeper.

If you want any proof of that, take for instance our attitude toward death, how we camouflage death, how we can not stand even the surface awareness of death. When I say we camouflage death, we also tend to camouflage birth. I am under the impression there are many young girls today who have the idea that with modern methods of having a child, you get a drug as soon as the thing is a little uncomfortable. When you wake up you have your baby wrapped in cellophane and presented by a nice nurse. We don't have the feeling that birth is a rather elementary act, something which isn't so easy, something which is not produced in the way of industrial production where something comes out of a machine.

We camouflage every other direct experience with reality. I am sure, for instance, that one reason why the latest movies of Chaplin have been so unpopular is simply because people are afraid of being touched that closely. *The Great Dictator* [1938–1940] ended with one of the most moving speeches I have ever heard. Most of the audience, even if they liked the picture, said: "No, that was not good, that was not artistic." I think they are not so concerned about something actually being too artistic. It got too close. *Monsieur Verdoux* [1944–1946] got very close, and I think the *Limelight* [1952] gets very close again, but this is much too strong for our audiences, so the critics rationalize. I read recently that the American Legion is threatening to boycott this movie in the west, and that the theatre owners have already started to cancel their orders for the film. I think American Legion can do this kind of thing only because there is indeed so much fear, so much phobia in the public against being brought in touch with themselves, with something they feel, with the reality of human existence. That what is perhaps one of the great expressions of American culture today can be boycotted, prevented from appearing by a pressure group, because it has not enough meaning, not enough attraction for the vast majority of people.

Instead of being related, being in touch with love, with hate, with fear, with doubt, with all of the basic experiences of man, we all are rather detached. We are related to an abstraction which is to say we are not related at all. We live in a vacuum and fill the vacuum, fill the gap with words, with abstract signs of values, with routine, which helps us out from the embarrassment.

There is one other thing we do, and that is, we are sentimental. What is *sentimentality*? I think there are probably a number of ways one can look at it, but I want to speak about one which has a certain connection with the topic I am talking about. I should like to describe *sentimentality is feeling under the condition of complete detachment.* Unless you are really insane, you have feeling, but if you are as detached, as remote, as unrelated to things as I was just talking about, then you have a very peculiar situation. You have feelings, but you do not refer really, concretely to something which is the reality. You are sentimental. Your feelings overflow. They appear somewhere. We use catch words, honesty, patriotism, or on the other hand words like revolution, or any number of words which are abstract concepts, which at the moment have no concrete meaning, but they are stimulation words, which make you weep, which make you howl, which make you do anything, and yet it is a performance in which the feeling is not really related to something with which you are concerned, but which is an empty thing.

It like a person crying the movies when the heroine loses a chance to make $100,000 and people cry and the same people in real life can witness a great tragedy around themselves and around their own lives, and they don't cry, and don't feel anything, because they are really unrelated. They are not concerned. They live in that vacuum of abstraction, of alienation from reality of feelings. Yet they have feelings, so what else can they do? There are some catch words, some stimuli, some situations provoking this feeling, but not in the sense that I cry because I am really related to unhappiness, but I am quite detached. I live in a vacuum, but the feeling that is in me needs some outlet, and so I cry where there is some occasion without really being related to anything, and I think that is the essence of sentimentality which can be observed so frequently in modern culture.

Sentimental people give the impression of being rather detached, rather remote, of not being related to anything particularly, and then you find these outbursts of feeling. You can see it in the movies, at a football game or at some other occasion where suddenly there is great emotion, great excitement, or great what seems joy, or great what seems sadness in their faces, and yet you can see that this facial expression is at the same time vacuous, empty. Here is a great difference between the person who experiences joy in a state of relatedness to something, and a person who has this kind of sentimental joy because there is some situation where his sense of joy is touched somewhere, but he is still perfectly detached from everything. He doesn't feel.

## e) Mental health and being related

All this state of abstraction, of being alienated from the concreteness of one's own experience, has far-reaching consequences for one's mental health, because what is the source of energy from which we live? Well, you might say there is one source of energy which is purely physical, which is rooted in the chemistry of our body, and we know that that energy is on the decline after the age of twenty-five. After that, we are slowly running down, as far as that source of energy is concerned. There is another source of energy, and that is the energy which springs from our being related to the world, our being concerned. You can experience it sometimes when you are with somebody whom you love, or when you read something which is intensely interesting, exciting. Then you don't get tired. You feel energy coming up which is unexpected. You feel a deep sense of joy, and if you watch some people at the age of eighty who have lived a life of intense relatedness, love, concern, interest actually you will see the surprising and overwhelming fact of a freshness and an energy there which has nothing to do with the body chemistry, with the sources which they have at their disposal.

Joy, energy, happiness, all this depends on the degree to

which we are related, to which we are concerned, and that is to say, to which we are in touch with the reality of our feelings, with the reality of other people, and not to experience them as abstractions which we can look at like the commodities at the market; and secondly, in this process of being related, we experience ourselves as entities, as I who is related to the world. I become one with the world in my relatedness to the world, but I also experience myself as a self, as an individuality, as something unique, because in this process of relatedness, I am at the same time the subject of this activity, of this process, of relating myself. I am I and I am the other person. I become one with the object of my concern, but in this process, I experience myself also as a subject.

When something is done in order to avoid boredom, or something is done out of relatedness or concern with something you can observe or sense the different. You have spent an evening with friends, and you have talked for the whole evening. Try to watch how you feel when you leave. Do you feel happy, alive, pleasant, good, or do you feel kind of tired and bored, or not even bored but a little bit dissatisfied and a little bit depressed, and you just have the feeling, "Well, all right. Thank God I can go to bed now." Even if it is late but you have enjoyed yourself, you feel alive, feel kind of happy, then you know that what you have been doing is not just to avoid boredom.

## f) Alienation and boredom

In a culture where we become alienated from ourselves, from others, in which our own human feelings become abstractions, cease to be concrete, we become awfully *bored*. We lose energy. Life ceases to be exciting in a true sense. I believe that boredom is one of the great evils which can befall man. There are few things which are as terrifying and unbearable as being bored.

When we get to be bored, we have certain ways of escaping from it. We start to go to parties, or to play bridge, or to drink or to work, or to drive around, or to do any number of things which help alleviate boredom. To refer to the example I gave in the first lecture, it seems to me that perhaps in certain cultures in which life is on the one hand quite comfortable, nevertheless in which boredom has developed to a large extent, one finds more cases of suicide and schizophrenia than in other countries in which there is at least more touch with reality, even if the reality is tragic, because sadness and tragedy are still easier to bear than boredom, which is nothing but the expression of an unrelatedness to the world and to love.

I would say that boredom is perhaps the word for a more normal average experience which in pathology would be called depression and melancholia. *Boredom is the average state of melancholia, while melancholia is the pathological state of boredom which one finds in certain individuals.* I think however, there is only a quantitative difference, and maybe the people who become melancholic have less good defenses to contend with the boredom of life than the majority of sane people who are bored, and know how to evade it and not to experience it consciously.

Of course one of the best ways of overcoming boredom is *routine.* If you have a schedule starting with your radio at seven in the morning down to twelve o-clock at night, and there is no minute which can not easily be killed, then you simply have no time to be bored. All that is necessary because boredom is unbearable only if you have time for it, so if you arrange a day in which you have no time left, you need not be bored. If that were not the case, then indeed we would have to build mental hospitals for the millions within a very short time.

## g) Alienation in politics

There is one last point I want to speak about in this connection. Not only our interpersonal communication, not only our relationship to ourselves, not only our relationship things is abstractified, but also our relationship to politics. We have a tradition which started out as a negation of the absolute state, namely that the individual citizen had a right to determine what should be done with the taxes he paid, and eventually a right to participate responsibly in the decision making about the fate of society. That is perfectly alright, and that was something very concrete. If you take a small community as there still exists in Switzerland, where a few thousand or a few hundred people gather together, they have concrete problems which they an overlook, discuss them, and these five hundred or a thousand people make a decision about something, then we know something concrete really has gone on. A decision has been made. There was nothing about it.

I may remind you of the fact that Aristotle discussed the question how large can a city be. It can not be smaller than a thousand, but certainly it could not be greater than ten thousand. Well a city of ten thousand people is still something very concrete. That is manageable. There decision making in a democratic sense, makes sense concretely. But what has become of our system in states where we have fifty million, two hundred fifty million people? It doesn't really make any difference whatsoever, just as little as if you say our budget is fifty billion or seventy billion. Obviously, all these figures lose any sense of concreteness. While we may handle ten thousand dollars, or one hundred thousand dollars, and maybe somebody can handle even a million in a concrete fashion, certainly the concept of fifty million is a purely abstract formula. It is a mathematical formula which gives you very correctly, a certain quantitative measurement but it is not related to anything you can grasp, just as you can not grasp distances between various stars more than in a sense of a perfectly abstract picture.

It happens that we are voting once in a while. Actually this voting is influenced to a large extent by practices which are very similar to modern advertising, in which catch words, nowadays by television, are brought to us. We are influenced to a large extent by emotional and completely irrational appeal. We behave to some extent as we behave toward a football game or boxing match, with that sense of drama which I was talking about last tine, namely it is exciting to see two candidates fight with each other, and to be able to sway the thing in some sense, to have a part in it. In a boxing match there is nothing we can do except sit and wait, while in these elections, there is something we can do. Even if our vote is very little, it is just a little bit in which we enter into the arena and have some influence.

But is that a responsible expression of our opinion? What do we know? What information do we have? Is not the whole sphere much too complicated to be decided on by the way in which we vote? Would there not be an entirely different way of discussion, of formulation, of opinion and of conviction if we were to make voting something really concrete? I think our present system of voting is still better than anything else which exists in the earth, but I think it is a very imperfect thing. It has become rather abstract. I shall try in the next lecture to say a few words in what direction I believe progress away from this kind of abstraction or abstractification is possible.

Actually, with all our sense of the participation of the citizen in the affairs of society, realistically speaking, concretely speaking, the individual citizen has very little chance to influence things; so you vote, which is in a sense deciding between *Chesterfields* and *Camels*. This is exaggerated and overdrawn, but at this moment, I would rather overdraw the picture, in order to make it clear, than to be too precise. You vote. You can write a letter to Congress. You can write a letter to your Senator, but actually, you will find that the vast majority of people have a feeling that there is almost nothing in which they can really, concretely and not abstractly influence and participate in the affairs of society. It is a process somewhere very remote from them and just as alienated and just as abstract, just as not concrete, as all the other things I have been talking about.

I should like to make one theoretical remark. One says in general, that in order to act, you must be able to think. First comes thought, and then comes reasonable action. I am sure that is true, but something else is true too, namely the reverse. Unless you have a possibility to act, you are greatly hindered in your thinking, that thinking develops only where there is at least a chance to apply it. If you take the owner of a small delicatessen store, I think he is much more intelligent in the affairs of his store, where he can act, where he can influence things, where he can observe and make decisions and do something with all his decisions, than he is in affairs of the state. The reason is not necessarily that affairs of the state are so much more difficult than the affairs of his store. I think sometimes they are awfully simple, and the affairs of the store can be very difficult. I don't think that it requires really more intelligence to think about foreign policy than to think about how much cheese to buy. The processes are pretty much the same, but in the one case you are able to, and therefore you can think, and in the other case, your avenue of influence, of acting is so reduced that you just talk. You talk in empty terms, but you don't think, and you feel rather resigned that your thinking doesn't serve any purpose.

To sum up: The general picture of our modern culture is one of a mode of production and consumption centering around the market, centering around mass production. That in itself is an abstractification and one of the great steps of progress in the development of economy. But at this point this method of production, this method of abstractification, has reached such proportions that it affects not only the technical sphere, but that all participants have been molded by it, that all experiences inside and outside of ourselves become abstract as commodities become in the market. We are unrelated to real experience, we are in a vacuum, we are therefore insecure, we are therefore in danger of boredom, and we are therefore in a very serious situation of mental health, which we only overcome by a routine in which we do not have to face our boredom and the emptiness of our relationship to others and to ourselves, and the abstract quality of our experiences.

# (FOURTH LECTURE: FEBRUARY 4, 1953)

## h) Alienated thinking

I was talking last time about what I called the alienation from oneself, from other people, from things, and the connection of this process of alienation with what I call the abstractification, that attitude which is characteristic for our modern industrial capitalist culture. In this culture we experience things, people, oneself, not in their concrete form, not in their use value, but in their abstract form, one of which is money, another of which is words, and to relate ourselves to these abstractions rather than to that which is real and concrete.

I should like to go a little further into other factors which are influenced by this process of alienation. What does it do to our *thinking*? I think we can compare it to what this alienation does to our feeling. I said last time that what happens is that we become sentimental, rather than to feel, and I tried to define sentiment as feeling under the condition of unrelatedness, that the feeling flows over, but it is empty because there is a need to feel, but nothing the feeling is related to. Something similar happens to our reason, or to our thought processes, if we are not related to that which we think about. To put it differently: If we are not concerned, then all that is left of our thought processes is intelligence. By intelligence, I mean an ability to manipulate concepts, but not to penetrate through the surface to the essence of things, to manipulate rather than to understand. This faculty of understanding, one might call reason, in contradistinction to manipulating intelligence. Reason indeed operates only if we are related to that which we think about. If we are unrelated to it, then we can do nothing but to manipulate. We can weigh and count and figure and compare factors. You might say this kind of intelligence has the very same character of abstractification which our feeling and our sensing has.

Reason might be a luxury sometimes, but sometimes the life of individuals and the life of mankind may depend on the ability to use reason in a penetrating sense and not only to use it in the sense of manipulation of purely intellectual, superficial thought process which never penetrate to anything and therefore never change anything.

All this is connected with our old *concept of science*. The scientific attitude is indeed one of the great achievements of the last few hundred years. What was this scientific attitude? It was an attitude of objectivity. It was a human attitude in which one had humility, in which one had the strength to look at the world objectively that is to say, as it is and not distort it by our own wishes and fears and imagination; it was a human attitude, where one had the courage to see and examine whether the data which we found confirmed our idea or disproved it, and whether one had the courage to change a theory if the data showed that they had not proven it. That was the essence of scientific thinking. It is really the ability to be surprised at something, to wonder. Most great scientific discoveries have really started at one point where a man does not take for granted what all have taken for granted before. At one point he wondered. He was surprised, and this is the scientific discovery. After that, the process is secondary. He studies, examines, makes tests, does all sorts of things, but the real genius of discovery is not in all this so-called scientific work which he does later. The real source of the scientific discovery is that moment when he was capable of wondering about something which nobody else wondered about so far.

It is very strange what goes on today. In the physical sciences, which are the most, or the only advanced ones today, you have this scientific attitude. You have tremendous effort, tremendous work, thought, and great uncertainty. But what is the opinion of the average person, what is the feeling about science, and not only of the average person, but also of most social scientists? They think that scientific thinking gives that which religion used to give a few hundred years ago, namely complete certainty. They can not tolerate uncertainty. For them science has become a new religion, a new certainty about facts of life, which gives them the sense of security which in another age, religion was to give.

The average person has become the consumer of science. He expects that the scientist knows it all, and that by reading the newspaper, he has about the same position as the man who goes to church. The priests are the specialists for handling relationships with God. For some people it is enough that they exist. You can see them from time to time, and I think in the contemporary attitude toward science, you find something very similar. People are convinced that they are the high priests of science who have complete certainty about the world. As long as they teach at universities, and the newspapers write about them, everything is all right. There is somebody at least who has certainty and conviction, and one feels a sense of security oneself.

What one really means by scientific approach, both the layman and the social scientist, is essentially something which is done by manipulating intelligence. It is taken for a scientific approach to a psychological problem if one can express it in abstract figures, if you counts, if you measure, even if your basic data doesn't make any sense and has no meaning whatsoever. Let me give you an example of this, how it operates in psychology. I read recently an article on a study of attitudes of mothers toward children. The mother was observed with the newborn infant who was brought to her in the first week after birth. There were three psychologists who observed what was going on. The basic data they referred to were, mother smiles, or mother pats the child on the head. These were taken as symptoms of a loving attitude. Then you had a very elaborate statistical apparatus based upon that, with possible error, and what not, in which all figures were given, how the percentages of the various types of mothers were divided in each group and so forth—except that your basic data is completely unscientific, because if you state, "Mother smiles," you know nothing about. It all depends on how she smiles. She can smile lovingly, bitterly, indifferently. She can pat the child on the head out of sheer boredom, annoyance or any number of things. So actually you do not use a scientific method in psychology because you do not actually describe, observe in detail the picture of what goes on in the greatest specificity and concreteness. You observe superficially and give it the appearance of a scientific endeavor by using this unscientific data with an alleged scientific method because it deals with figures.

No theoretical physicist, no chemist would get away with that. He would not even get away with such a method in his second year in college, because it is a thoughtless method which is faking science. But there seems to be a kind of gentlemen's agreement among social scientists. As long as you use figures and statistical methods, your data is scientific.

## i) Alienated loving

Finally I want to talk about another problem which is also related, namely what happens to *love* in this situation of self alienation, of unrelatedness? I think what we see is that love is, so to speak, divided into two channels; one, it becomes identified with sex, and you get the many books in which you learn sexual techniques in order to enhance love in marriage; or love becomes a rather sexless unerotic thing in which two people get along well with each other, and if they happen to be a woman and a man, they get married, and call that love. It is nice companionship at best, but there is not much of any spark, of any particular glowing element, which in older times was connected with the idea of love.

Under these conditions of unrelatedness, love is experienced as identified with sex, or identified with getting along, is identified with a rather routine pleasant companionship, which is lacking, and quite naturally lacking under these circumstances, in the concept and fact of *tenderness*. Look for expressions of tenderness in a Hollywood movie. You rarely find it. You can find it in a French movie. You can find it to an exceptional degree in a Chaplin movie. Tenderness is more than sex and more than a pleasant getting along, but is an expression of loving relatedness to another person, not only the sense of individual love, but even in the sense of love for man as such.

It is quite logical and quite natural that in a culture like ours, tenderness has been reduced to almost zero as an experience. I am afraid that what is even worse is that many people feel it and are kind of ashamed because it does not seem to be anything.

Maybe one is afraid of being a sissy, or childish or a sucker or not living up to the picture of the passionate man or woman, if anyone shows tenderness.

There is a good deal of talk in recent years that we might understand how vicious we are. Dr. Niebuhr emphasizes the viciousness of man, that it is very important to be aware of the destructiveness and viciousness which is part of our nature. I don't mean to go into a theoretical or analytic argument with Dr. Niebuhr, but it seems to me that our problem, at least in our culture at present is not that people are so vicious and destructive. What we can see in the United States on the whole, is a rather remarkable absence of destructiveness and viciousness and in fact, most people are rather kind and well-meaning and not destructive at all.

I think the trouble is something else, namely our *indifference*, our lack of concern, our not making a decision between life and death, our going along and living without knowing what for, our indifference to ourselves and to the future. I think that is a much more serious problem and perhaps we flatter ourselves to think we are such devils as Dr. Niebuhr believes, that we are so destructive and vicious. That would be something; perhaps. I think in a sense it is worse. We are just indifferent. We are just not concerned. I am afraid that is, in a way, more dangerous than the viciousness, but at least one can say that there are certain dangers to this emphasis on the viciousness of man because it seems to detract from that which is our real problem, our indifference.

# 4. WAYS TO OVERCOME INSANE SOCIETY

## a) Socialist's vision and its distortion

Are there solutions different from the ones which our present system offers us? We all know that there is one solution which has been victorious over various parts of the world: the totalitarian solution. Totalitarianism has created a new pagan religion, regressing far behind the beginnings of Christianity, in which we find a mixture of hero worship, worship of work, fear, terror, all that mixed together into a frightful system of a pagan religion. We all know by now that these things are very bad and no particular purpose is served to go on and on and to say how terribly inhuman the Russian system is. If one has to say it so often, one might even suspect that one didn't quite believe it. So let us go on to something else, namely to a more constructive solution which has been important not so much in the United States, but in Europe and in Asia, the solution of socialism.

The common vision to various socialists, the schools which arose in the nineteenth century or even somewhat earlier, was a society where man is an end in himself, where the individual citizen is active, responsible, where he lives with his fellow man in a spirit of cooperation, solidarity and brotherly love, where he is not used by anybody nor does he use himself for any purpose outside of his own life and the growth of his personality. In a way this common goal of all socialist schools is very closely related to what you might call the Messianic idea of the Old Testament. I want to say a few words about it.

You can not quite understand the Messianic idea without going back to a rather early point in history, namely the story of creation. What happens in the so-called "Fall of Adam and Eve?" We find here an assumption that man originally lived in complete harmony with nature being part of nature, but without awareness of himself, without consciousness of himself, without knowledge of good and evil. God forbids man to eat from the tree of knowledge of good and evil and he does anyway. Suddenly he sees himself separate from nature, separate from each other; man and woman see each other naked and they are ashamed. They feel their separation. They feel the alienation between them and what is called "God's Curse." "God's Curse" is that man shall be man's enemy, one sex the other sex's enemy, and man shall be the enemy of nature, of animals, and of the fruit of the fields. At this point human history begins.

According to the prophetic version of the Messianic concepts, the aim of history is to arrive at a new harmony between man and man, and man and nature, but a new harmony not any more on the basis of man being part of nature without being aware of himself, but on the basis of man's development of reason, his awareness of himself, his love, to such an extent that he will be capable one day of creating a new harmony between himself and nature, and between man and man, in which there is no more war and in which there is abundance. According to this prophetic tradition, the Messianic age is a fulfillment on a higher level of what was a Paradise Age on a primitive level. Paradoxically enough, in this concept of the Messianic Age, man is right against God. God had forbidden him to eat from the fruit of knowledge. Man has done it anyway and knows he is on the way of creating something which is higher, and better then that which he had left.

That is essentially the prophetic version of the Messianism, and that is essentially the idea common to all socialists of the nineteenth century, a new harmony, a harmony created on the basis of knowledge, love, solidarity, which would create also abundance and destroy the fight between man, or do away with the fight between man and nature, and man and man. This was the general idea. But there were many schools of thought in socialism which differed with regard to the means which they thought were necessary to attain this ideal. Some schools emphasized from the very beginning, the necessity of avoiding the danger of centralization emphasized the dangers which were to be fundamental in the organization of the state and any great power the state would have. The Marxist socialists on the other hand, believed that one had to conquer the state as an instrument which was capable and necessary to transform society into a classless society and in the last analysis stateless society of free men.

The Marxist socialists furthermore thought that the means to this end of freeing and liberating man was the socialization of the means of production. The idea was that if the means of production were not in the hands of one person any more, if they were the property of all, then there would be nobody who could exploit or manipulate the worker. They had the rather naive idea that while the socialization of the means of production was not an end in itself, it was the means by which rather immediately a transformation of man into responsible, cooperative people would follow.

On an intellectual scale, Marxist socialism won out against all other groups. It won out in Europe, in Russia, in China, provided we call that Marxist socialism (but that is another question which I may touch on in a minute). It lost out in the United States, but no other group won either.

What had been the Marxist criticism of capitalism? It was essentially criticism on an economic level. The criticism was a two-fold one, in the first place, that in the capitalist system the worker is exploited. He has to work long hours and for small wages and that he can not and will not participate in the increasing worth of society to the same degree in which those who own capital participate. The second criticism was that capitalism by its mode of production, is not capable of using the productive forces of society sufficiently. It is not capable of avoiding crises, of avoiding war, and serves, by its particular way of organization to paralyze and to hinder the development of the productive forces which already exist in society.

This was essentially a criticism from the economic angle. It refers to man primarily from the standpoint that the working class remained exploited, poor, suffering, and only in the younger writings of Marx or here and there later, do you find concepts which refer not to material need, to suffering, but which refer to those very concepts of alienation, to the concept of the declining of man to that which happens to man in a much more sudden and profound way than just material need. But while Marxism in many ways recognized and mentioned it, it was more or less lost in the further development of Marxian socialism, which retained as its criticism of the capitalist system, essentially the economic criticism.

Quite obviously, this criticism against capitalism proved to be inaccurate. Certainly the American development, and to some extent the Western European development proved that Marx's view that with the development of capital, the worker would remain suffering, exploited, without participating in the increasing wealth of society, simply was not true. We see in the United States a tremendous increase in earning, in social prestige, in political power of the working class, and the picture of the ever increasingly exploited, impoverished workers even in relative terms, is certainly in quite a contrast with the American reality of the development of capitalism.

Secondly, American capitalism and to some extent the capitalism of other countries has shown a much greater ability to develop productive forces than Marxists predicted. It is always possible to say that with another system it could have developed more, but it sounds rather theoretical to say that. We are just stunned by the tremendous dimension of increasing production which we see in the United States in the last ten, twenty years.

Obviously, the structure of capitalism has changed tremendously since the days of Marx. It is a capitalism which, especially in the United States, under the "New Deal," has integrated many things which were originally socialist demands, in which the working class has been integrated as an integral part of capitalist economy, and in which certainly no particular impression is made on anybody in the old argument of socialists that capitalism is a hinderance for production and that under capitalism workers starve. But my main criticism of socialist theory of past and present, is not the wrong diagnosis made economically. Why should this scientific theory which Marx developed a hundred years ago, have been accurate, why should he have foreseen developments which happened a hundred years later? These mistakes don't have anything to do with the scientific method which Marx used.

My criticism of the economic theory and concepts of socialism as it was used in the last fifty years, refers to something else. One has less and less criticized capitalism for what it does to man, for the effect it has on life, not in an economic sense, but in the sense of stultifying and diminishing intensity of feeling, of making man into a commodity, and of all the effects I have been talking about in these lectures? That is something which capitalism does not only to the worker. It does it to everybody who is enmeshed in this system.

If one is concerned with man, as the one aim of one's concern, then indeed the criticism of capitalism should not be the one of the suffering it causes in the obvious economic sense. Capitalism shows all signs that eventually this suffering can be taken care of and dealt with, but should be criticized of what this mode of production and consumption, this mode of social organization does to man's soul, to man's life, to man's feeling, to man's concept of himself. Not only did the socialist theory not criticize capitalism essentially from this viewpoint. It also did not develop a clear vision of what socialism could be and ought to be, beyond the mere smoother functioning of economy.

If we ask what is the reason for the defeat of the socialists in the United States and Europe, I would think here lies at least one of the main reasons for its defeat. It appealed only to economic interests and ignored the fact that the ideal interests of man, his need for a frame of reference, his need for an object of devotion, are as great or I think greater than his economic interests are. The economics interests of the working class are and were taken care of pretty well by the trade unions. The socialist movement in many ways did not add very much to that, except giving some political power to the trade unions, very often also being their prisoner. But the socialist movement failed to create a sense of a new human vision, and if you please, of a new religion.

There has been a very interesting paper written by Julian Huxley and presented by him at the occasion of the last Humanistic Congress in Amsterdam last summer [1952]. There he posed the question whether we are not in need of a new humanist religion. He presented ideas which are pretty similar to the ones I have suggested here: We have to define religion in the broadest sense of the word, not referring specifically to theistic religion; we have to recognize that man has to have a frame of reference, an object of devotion, that he has to have meaning to life; we have to have an objective which goes beyond that of producing and reproducing himself. Huxley suggested the question that while we could not create a religion artificially, at least we could indulge in ideas whether and how such a new form of non-theistic humanistic religion is possible. There are all over the world today attempts here and there to recreate religion in the one or the other form. There exist quite a few in America in various forms. I think this all bears witness to a very deep need to create a vision, to create a picture of new forms of human relationship and of symbols which stand for these new forms.

It seems to me that socialism had to fail if it was not capable of providing such a vision. It had to fail, if it did not offer something more than a proposed solution on the economic plane, if it could not appeal to the deepest longing in man and especially to that which is frustrated and not satisfied in our modern system. That Stalinism and that Fascism could become so strong and could become victorious in many countries, I am sure is due to the fact that vicious as the system is, it offers something in terms of a new religion, in terms of devotion which socialism failed to offer, simply continuing with the trend of thought which was plausible and which was existing a hundred or even seventy or eighty years ago.

There is one particular point which I want to mention

where I believe that socialist theory took a wrong turn, so to speak: the assumption that the most urgent task in society was the aim of socializing the means of production. We have socialization of the means of production in Russia completely and we can see empirically that this socialization of the means of production has not lead to freedom or to any of the aims of socialism, but to a state capitalism in which the enslavement of the worker and of every man is greater than even the worst kinds of modern capitalism. We have a good deal of socialization of the means of production in England. Is the life, is the position of the worker in Britain any different if he works on a railroad where his manager is nominated by the state or whether he is a man nominated by the Board of Directors? His actual function in work, his real role concretely speaking is pretty much the same and it seems to me that the emphasis of socialism, that the solution in each country ought to be the socialization of the means of production, failed to see that this formula is not sufficiently concrete. This end does not really keep a promise which it was thought it would keep, namely to be the condition for free, cooperative work of man. In fact, this aim is still today the main political aim of all socialist parties, which seems to me very exasperating, because they aim for something which when achieved does not lead to anything.

What the socialist program ought to be concerned with, as far as I can see, are changes in the function of the worker, changes in the function of working conditions, and changes in our political structure. I want at the moment to mention two more points of criticism of socialist tradition. One is an obvious disregard for the world outside of Europe and America. Socialism always speaks of it as a world movement, as an international movement. What it really meant was only Europe. It is quite interesting and significant that one of these last weeks, the socialists of India and other countries met and formed an organization of their own in which for the first time adapted socialism as a demand and says very clearly that internationalism must mean something much more than what European socialists meant by it, which was essentially a European affair. As long as one was thinking essentially in European terms one had a rather difficult problem to think of than if one were thinking of universal problems. China and India as one of the most crucial problems in developing the resources of the world and a problem which had been practically neglected by the socialists in attempting to find a solution.

There is eventually one other point which I want to mention: a distorted socialist theory, that the new millennium would arrive in our time. The whole theory was kind of pushed into the straightjacket of this assumption, to fit it, and to prove that the new socialist society, a new age for mankind will be achieved now. Therefore all data one collected had to be distorted in such a way as to prove this point. This was the one attitude which you found in Marx, which you found in Lenin, and which probably is one of the factors which drove Russian communism in the direction of the very opposite socialism ever stood for. Then there was the other attitude which I found in some socialist parties of other countries, namely an endless patience based on a scientific predilection of how things had to be, and the attitude would work that there was nothing one had to do in particular but wait, and things would take care of themselves.

Socialism was torn into these two poles, the historical implications which led to great errors and later to crimes and historical indolence and kind of patience which led to a passivity which permitted in Germany the fascists to win. I would say that there is such a thing which you might call the Messianic paradox by which I mean to be patient and impatient at the same time, to know that one can not force the end but also not to sit unconcerned and to wait for the laws of history to determine this end.

There is an old Jewish story of a Rabbi who spoke to the Messiah and asked him when he would come and he said "Tomorrow." He went back and expected him, and when he didn't come he was very furious at the Messiah for having lied. He expressed his anger to the Prophet Elijah who said: "You are quite mistaken. He didn't lie. He said tomorrow and that was true, but he meant if you want him, if you are ready, if you are willing."

This paradox has always existed in the Messianic attitude of being capable of waiting but not of becoming indolent, of not forcing the end but not having the kind of patience which ceases to be concerned. What happened to socialism, is that the two poles of this Messianic paradox became torn apart. There was on the one hand an impatience which turned to crime, and on the other hand, a patience which also turned into a crime but perhaps of a lesser nature.

## b) What can be done?

I shall try to say a few words at least to indicate what could be done.

In the first place I think it is most necessary for us to overcome the discouragement of and loss of faith which progressive forces are suffering from now increasingly in the last ten years. I don't think that even Senator [Joseph Raymond] McCarthy is a figure which ought to wipe out all the hopes for human improvement and progress which the human race has had for a few thousand years. There is a jitteriness about all these things which is not quite realistic, but which is partly the expression of a loss of faith which has gone on and which one can understand as a result of a great disillusionment of people who thought that progress was around the corner. In order to quote Spinoza in a slightly different way: If this end would be so easy to achieve, it would have been achieved a long time ago, so apparently the progress of the human race is slow. I don't think there is any reason to believe that the epoch in which we live is one of decay and is one which has turned the clock of humanity backwards.

We live in an age which has done things which are really new in the history of mankind. That can not be said so often about any age. We have made a tremendous progress in thought which can be compared with the great periods of Greece in the five hundred years before Christ, with the great periods of the beginning of the modern age and certainly this progress and its achievements are not symptoms of a decaying age. We can visualize the fulfillment of one of the oldest dreams of mankind, namely such an increase in wealth that the material needs of man can be satisfied and we certainly can visualize that even in a few generations, this problem will be more unified than even today. This had been a vision, an ideal, a hope, but only now one begins to visualize as a reality.

Aside from all that, there are even signs that there is a growing awareness in the United States, and in many other countries that in this whole process we have lost something, in trying to build machines which we must be very concerned to regain. I think this kind of progressive reaction has already begun and is something which is ever increasing. So I don't see any reason to get suddenly so pessimistic about the human race. Besides that, it is really a rather egocentric and unobjective standpoint to measure history in terms of our life span. A few hundred years, historically speaking, are certainly very little. Probably we are right now at the point which later on will be described as the end of the Middle Ages and these four hundred years will be remembered as such.

It is necessary that we become aware of where our progress has led us astray, where our government which in itself was a progressive development, has led to human consequences which we must change if we want to enjoy the fruits of this progressive development.

There is to change basic things in our social and political situation. That seems to me is the real problem of socialism, not that primarily of the socialization of the means of production. The problem of socialism is that of *socializing conditions of work, functions of the worker*, in which the individual person can become an active cooperative person in his work, in which work becomes dignified and meaningful again, an expression of the life force of a person. What the social changes and means would be to achieve this end is that which we must study and seems to me is the real problem of socialism. Parallel to this problem is a change in our political structure in the direction of *making democracy work*, to make it something concrete. We are confronted with the fact that today the individual citizen, practically speaking, has almost no possibility to influence events which go on. We know little. We are not asked. Decisions are made which have to be made above our heads in the kind of system which we operate, but the question is: Can means and ways be found to organize work, to organize society, to organize government in such a way that people are not handled and manipulated like automatons, but that individual citizens can have a chance to participate in decisions.

Partly this problem amounts to the question, is our industrial system of production compatible with individuality? Can one produce in a way of mass production, can one have highly centralized big enterprises and at the same time have an individualism and an emphasis on man's individual responsibility and participation which I am speaking about?

It is absurd to say that we will do away with the developments of the industrial age. We won't, because quite obviously the advantage of freeing man from the burdens of physical work and of giving him means to live and not to suffer are so obvious that mankind will not do away with the achievements of the last four hundred years. Granted also, that it is indeed very difficult to combine an industrial system with a social system of democracy and individualism, but I wonder whether the solution of this problem is more difficult than the production of the atom bomb. I imagine the tremendous amount of thought and work and effort which has been put in physics into the production of the atom bomb, and I imagine the almost complete lack of thought and effort which has been put into these questions of how one could create a system in which our industrial system would be compatible with a democratic individualist system. Only if one had tried a thousand times more than our social scientists, our politicians and all of us have tried, even only then could one have the right to speak of difficulty. So far we haven't even tried, and I don't see any particular reason why the solution of this problem should be more difficult than the solution of the problems in the natural sciences, provided we see its significance and provided we are really concerned.

There is a distinction between the way in which a society is organized, its production is organized, its work is organized, and the way people are. I believe that certain basic and fundamental changes are necessary in order to give man the possibility for a more human individual existence: But I believe also that we must begin with ourselves. If one talks about politics and social change without beginning to examine one's own attitude, without changing something in oneself, then all of this is rather idle talk or dangerous because that which one aims at, which one wishes to produce is not related to an inner experience. Hence one cannot decide whether such a change is good or bad. I think it is just as dangerous to be caught in the abstract nature of our politics today as it is to be caught in the abstract danger of socialist ideologies. Certainly Stalinism has shown where this abstractification of some elements leads, that a system of complete terror and lack of freedom can still call itself socialism and democracy.

There is a sentence in the Old Testament which I think has some reference to our situation today. It says: "And you shall be cursed because thou did not serve thy God, in joy and gladness amidst the abundance of things." [Deuteronomium 28:47] We have an abundance of things but we serve them and without joy and gladness.

We have liberated forces of nature. We have liberated energies and are in the process of making them useful for the economic life of society, energies which one never knew about, and could never do anything about. Apparently in this process of liberating natural energies, we have suppressed and stultified more and more human energy. We can see in certain cases and in certain dramatic situations, that man has a sort of energy which is indeed as marvellous and surprising as the energy which physicists find in an atom, but human energy is bound almost completely. It does not find expression. It has not been liberated. It is to a large extent paralyzed. It seems to me that the task of the future is not only to look at the liberation of physical energy, but to look into ourselves, to see that such institutions are created and such changes are made personally and institutionally which make it possible for human energy to be liberated, and to be used in the process of living of society.

We have to keep our industrial mode of production, though

it leads to the alienation of man from himself and leads to all of the effects of mental unhappiness which we have been talking about. Therefore we have a problem, to combine centralization with decentralization. We have a problem to think about, to discover means of social organization of work, and organization of democracy which can combine the functioning of industrial machines with a much greater amount of individual initiative, participation, responsibility. This is a problem which is similar to the problem of the eighteenth century where one was confronted with the distribution of power. How could a democrats state operate? How could this function? This was at first a blueprint vision, scientific thought about the possibility of new social forms.

I think it is possible to develop modes of work, organization of industry and even some beginnings are in the United States. There is the experience of cooperatives all over the world. What I tried to say was the following:

If we see that this problem is one we have to solve, if we don't want to lose either the machine or man, if we apply our knowledge, our concern, our intelligence to this problem, it is not more difficult to solve than many of our scientific problems which we have solved. The trouble is not that it is so difficult to solve, that it can't be done, that there are any inherently impossible things. The trouble is we are just continuing with a scheme of things one hundred fifty or two hundred years old, and we are simply not paying attention to the fact that while it worked in many respects, in many human respects it does not work and works less and less well and might even destroy that which it once built up.

# II. The Concept of Mental Health

# 1. PREVAILING CONCEPTS OF MENTAL HEALTH

There are basically two concepts of mental health. One, one might call the society oriented one, and one I would call the man-oriented one—or to use another more familiar and more traditional word, a humanistic concept of mental health.

The *society-oriented concept of mental health* means that man is healthy if he can fulfill the functions which society gives him, if he can function according to the needs of any given society. Let me give you a special example. Assuming you have a primitive tribe which lives from attacking other tribes and killing their members and robbing what they have, and assuming there is one man who doesn't like it—that is to say, he is appalled by the idea of killing people and robbing. He will not be aware, probably of this dislike, because in this particular society it is just unthinkable to dislike what everybody likes. In fact, in every society it is always unthinkable to dislike what most people like.

Probably one morning when they go on the warpath, he will not be aware that he dislikes killing people, but he will have an attack of vomiting. Since they probably are not yet advanced enough to have psychiatrists, it will not be diagnosed as a psychogenetic illness or symptom, but certainly they will say—the medicine man or whoever it is—there is something very wrong with the man. Where everybody goes happily to attack the enemy, he starts vomiting, which prevents him from going to the attack. This man in sick in this society, while in a tribe of peaceful peasants, he is the one who would be very healthy. And, exactly the one who likes to kill would be the sick one in a cooperative society of peasants.

The humanistic concept of mental health is an entirely different one. It is one in which mental health is not determined by the proper functioning in any given society but is determined by criteria which are inherent in man. What that means, I shall talk about at some greater length later. If there were no conflict between the purposes of society and the purposes of the full development of man, then indeed the two concepts of mental health would be identical, and there would be no point in separating them. But, so far in history there has invariably been a conflict between the interests of individual development and the interests of any given society and therefore the two concepts of mental health have always been distinct and different. In fact, however, those who present the society-oriented concept of mental health always make it appear as if this concept is at the same time a man-oriented concept of mental health. In other words they always claim that that which is good, is best for their particular society is also good and best for man. And most people believe that.

The concept of mental health in the society-oriented form or person usually chooses a somewhat more polite word. It isn't exactly said that healthy is a man who fulfills a function of society, although that is said sometimes, but what is said, is for instance, a formula in which mental health consists in the capacity of man to work and to have pleasure. That sounds very innocuous, because who can deny that working and pleasure are good things for everybody? Or, they also might say mental health consists in the ability to produce and to reproduce their race. In the latter, pleasure would be mainly expressed by the sexual capacity of men and women. What we easily ignore in formulating it this way is, what kind of work is one talking about? Is one talking about interesting work, boring work, rewarding work? What kind of pleasure is one talking about? Is one talking about pleasure in which man forgets himself, like in alcoholism? Or the pleasure which is now so frequent in our modern Western society, the pleasure of the excitement of catastrophe? Of brutality? Or does one talk about the pleasures of joy, of aliveness of interesting things, of attractive work, of something which makes life interesting?

Such a formula of work and pleasure just doesn't make any sense. It has no meaning unless we define specifically what kind of work we mean and what kind of pleasure we mean. And therefore, like most of those generalized concepts, it only functions to hide the fact that while one is talking about man's work and pleasure one is actually talking about society's interest in having man function in certain ways. The same idea is often expressed in the way, that mental health means the adjustment of the individual to society. But again here we have the same problem, which one can express most rapidly by asking, is an individual sane when he is adjusted to an insane society?

There is another concept of mental health which is often used in psychiatry and which is not the society-oriented concept. It is very often, however, implicitly so, but not necessarily. This concept simply says that *mental health consists in the absence of mental illness*. That is to say, if there is no neurosis, no psychosis, no symptoms, and, if to speak on a more social level, there is no alcoholism, no homicide, no hopelessness, or relatively little, then we can speak of a relatively healthy individual or a relatively healthy society. This is the concept as it is used to a large extent in medicine in general. That is to say, the concept of health is largely in terms of the absence of illness, and it is only relatively recently—I remember and remind those of you who are familiar with the American literature, of the work of Dr. Dunn in Washington and others—that what we are really trying to discover is a concept of mental health, or of health in general, which is not defined negatively by absence of illness, but positively; namely by the presence of well being.

# 2. MENTAL HEALTH AND EVOLUTIONARY THINKING

The *humanistic concept of mental health* which I shall discuss now is a dynamic interpretation, and I should like to say a word about the peculiar quality of this dynamic interpretation of this concept as defined first in Freud. I have to stress that this concept in based on an evolutionary function as we find it in Darwin, Freud and Marx. That is to say,, the development of man in seen as an evolutionary development which can be traced back and which can be to some extent predicted. However, what is characteristic for Freud and what is characteristic for Marx, the two greatest representatives of evolutionary thinking in the social sciences, is that this evolutionary concept is connected with the concept of value. This is to say that the earliest stages are also less valuable, and the later, or, as they are often called, the higher stages are more valuable, from the standpoint of value, are better from the standpoint of value.

Now, that is a very complicated concept because it leads us into the following difficulty, which I shall try to exemplify by examples. You have an infant who is completely narcissistic, and you have an adult who is completely narcissistic. Is the infant sick? No, because the narcissism of the infant is a necessary part of his evolutionary development. In the course of his evolution, narcissism at an early stage is a necessary part. And, precisely because it is necessary, it is not pathological. If the person twenty years later shows the same degree of narcissism, he is psychotic. I could give another example. If a little child of three or four loves to play with his faeces, this in not pathological. If the adult twenty years later would have the same pleasure, this is a most ominous symptom of a mental illness.

Inasmuch as a certain phenomenon in necessary in a stage of human evolution, it in not pathological. If, however, it continues beyond its evolutionary necessity, then it becomes pathological. And, that is precisely what Freud describes, for instance, as being a "regression," or a "fixation." You find the very same idea in Marx's evolutionary thinking. Slavery, for instance, in not in itself morally evil as long as the development of society makes slavery a necessity. Or, that would hold true for property, that would hold true for alienation, and as on. If, however, slavery exists in a situation in which it is not necessary because the general conditions of society would permit the overcoming of slavery, then it becomes a pathological phenomenon.

Actually, in this lies the explanation for a famous sentence of Hegel, who held the same idea and on whom all his thinking in based, a statement by Hegel which is often misquoted. Hegel said: "What is real is rational." [G. W. F. Hegel, 1821, p. 24.] This has often been misquoted as saying that Hegel was such a reactionary that he accepted everything that existed; even the worst things were "rational," provided they existed. What Hegel meant in his own system by "real" was "real inasmuch as it is necessary." That is to say, that which is necessary in the evolutionary process is never pathological, but it becomes pathological if it exists beyond its evolutionary necessity. It is quite clear that in order to have such a concept, you need to have a clear concept of evolution; that is to say, which are the stages of evolution through which the individual, or mankind at large, have to pass. And clearly, if you see Freud, he has a very clear concept of the stages of evolution. Hegel has the same, and Marx to some extent also.

The Freudian concept is one which by and large defines mental health in two ways: one, mental health is achieved if the Oedipus complex has been overcome—that is to say, if the original fixation, the incestuous fixation toward the mother and the resulting hostility toward the father have been overcome; and secondly, if the libido has developed through the pre-genital stages and has arrived at the genital stage. This is a clear evolutionary concept based on the idea that human development begins with the Oedipus complex and in the pre-genital stages necessarily passes through this development, and the mentally healthy person can be defined as a person who has finished this process satisfactorily, who has gone satisfactorily through the stages of evolution.

# 3. MY OWN CONCEPT OF MENTAL HEALTH

I should like now to talk about my own concepts, which are based on Freud but which, however, emphasize certain things slightly more and in a slightly different way, although not really essentially. I should like to talk about *mental health here in terms of the overcoming of narcissism, or to speak positively, the resulting achievement of love and objectivity;* the overcoming of alienation (which is a Hegelian-Marxian concept and not a quantity found in Freud) and the resulting sense of identity and independence; the overcoming of hostility and the resulting capacity for peaceful life; and eventually, the achievement of productiveness, which means the overcoming of the archaic phases of cannibalism and of dependency.

When I think of the mental health of the individual I think mainly of the mental health of the society. I learned when I was a boy in school, and you probably did too, the old Latin saying, "*Mens sana in corpore sano,*" that a healthy mind exists in a healthy body. That is at best a half truth. There are many unhealthy minds in healthy bodies and many healthy minds in unhealthy bodies. But I think one may say with more correctness, "*Mens sana in societate sana,*" that a healthy mind—with exceptions of course—can exist only in healthy societies, and that therefore the problem of individual mental health and social mental health simply cannot be separated for man.

### a) Overcoming narcissism

Let me first talk about the overcoming of narcissism. I know that most of you are familiar with Freud's concept of narcissism, so I can be very brief in making a few explanations for those of you who might be less familiar with it. I should like to start out by saying that I believe that, perhaps, one of the greatest discoveries of Freud was precisely the discovery of this concept of narcissism, and that there is probably no entity which is more significant and more basic in the production of mental illness than narcissism. And, I would say that if I were forced to define mental health just in one sentence, I would say that mental health consists in the minimum of narcissism. But I shall try to be a little bit more concrete about it.

Freud means by narcissism an attitude in which that which is subjective, my own feelings, my physical needs, my other needs, have a great deal more reality than that which is objective, than that which is outside. The clearest example for it, of course, is to be found in the infant, especially in the newborn infant, and in the psychotic person. In the newborn infant there is no reality except the inner reality of needs. To a certain extent the outer world does not even exist, in terms of conceiving it. And the same holds true for a psychotic person. Psychosis is—if one wants to give it a general definition—is precisely the complete narcissism with the almost complete absence of relatedness to the world, objectively, as it is.

In between the infant and the psychotic are we, the so-called normal people, and as Freud has already observed, narcissism plays a considerable role in all of us, more or less. Let me give you an example: A man falls in love with a woman and she has absolutely no interest in him. He, if he is very narcissistic, will not be able to recognize that she is not interested. Because his logic says, and he will often say so, "How could it be that she doesn't love me if I love her so much?" The only reality for him is his own love. And that there is a person who might have different feelings, different reactions, is not for him a piece of reality.

You know the story of the author who meets a friend and talks about his book, I mean the author's book, and after fifteen minutes he says, "Well, now I've talked so much about myself, let us talk about you now." The friend says, "All right," and the author says, "How did you like my latest book?" Well, there you have the same narcissism, except that is already quite familiar. That is not as ominous and not as pathological as the first two examples.

Actually, the narcissistic person is simply not capable of conceiving the world emotionally in its own reality over there. He perceives it intellectually. If he didn't, he would be insane. But he does not perceive it emotionally. Because there is a confusion that is often made I want to say that narcissism, in the Freudian sense and in the sense in which I use it here is something quite different from egotism and vanity. A person can be very *egotistical*—you might say that always implies also a certain amount of narcissism, but not necessarily more than the average person—but he is egotistical in the sense he is not a loving person. He is not really very much interested in the world outside, but he wants everything for himself. But the very egotistical person may have a very good concept of the world outside. The *vain* person is usually, at least a certain kind of vanity, not a particularly narcissistic person.

He is usually a very insecure person, who needs confirmation all the time. So he will ask you all the time if you like him; if he is clever and psychoanalytically trained he will not do so outright; he will do it in a slightly indirect way. But actually what he is principally concerned with is—to be concerned with his own sense of insecurity. But that is not necessarily narcissistic. The truly narcissistic person doesn't give a damn what you think about him because there in no doubt that what be thinks about himself is real and that every word he says is just wonderful. And if you meet a really narcissistic person, and if he comes into a room and says, "Good morning," then he feels, "Isn't that wonderful." He is just there and says good morning. It's something beautiful for him.

The result of narcissism is the distortion of objectiveness and judgment because for the narcissistic person, "that is good which is mine and that is bad which is not mine." The second result is the lack of love because obviously I do not love anybody outside if I only am concerned with myself. And Freud has made a very significant remark here; that is, to what extent relations which seem like love, namely relations with children, and among people who are what they call love with each other. Actually this kind of relationship very often is only a narcissistic one. That is to say, in a mother's loving her children, she actually loved herself because they are her children; and the same, if she happens to love her husband, might go on with him. I would not say that this is necessarily so, but this is indeed very frequent and therefore very often that the narcissistic character of such a person is hidden behind the appearances, which are that of a loving attitude toward another person.

Another result you can observe if narcissism is disappointed within a person. Then you have two reactions: one of anxious depression and of rage. That depends on many factors. It is a very interesting problem psychiatrically to study to what extent psychotic depressions are the result of severe wounds to narcissism that the mourning of which Freud speaks as part of the depression is not the mourning over the image of the narcissistic ego which has been destroyed rather than the mourning over another person which has been incorporated. If you hurt the narcissistic person's feelings, you find a great deal of rage. Now, whether that rage is conscious or not depends mainly on the social position. If he has power, than probably his rage will be quite conscious. If you have power over him, he will not dare to have conscious rage, and you will find a depressed person. But maybe, once, if the situation changes, you will find a rage rather than a depression.

The overcoming of narcissism as the aim of life is expressed in phenomena which among themselves seem to be quite different, namely in the great religions of the East and West and in modern science. It is the aim of man to overcome his narcissism, to be able to love, to be able to overcome this worship of his own ego, and so on. And that is precisely the function of modern science, because modern science, aside from its results, as a human attitude is an attitude of accepting reality as it is, and not as I wish it to be.

Great hopes are connected with the development of modern science, that it would also lead to that attitude of objectivity and reason which is the essence of the overcoming of narcissism. It is very interesting, in fact, that the most outstanding modern scientists today, which I think are the theoretical physicists, are found among the sanest individuals which we find in the world, with some conspicuous exceptions which I shall not mention. And for me, this sanity today is to a large extent expressed by one thing, by the capacity of seeing that the nuclear arms race leads to disaster, and its utter folly. And there is probably no one in the world, no professional group in the world which has seen that with such clarity as the physicists. Unfortunately our own profession is not precisely in the first rank of this insight although one might say it should be there.

Because we are here interested not primarily in individuals' problems, but in social problems I must add a very important element: the change of narcissism from individual narcissism to group narcissism. You will find that the narcissistic individual is completely wrapped up with himself. Then you find sometimes the family narcissism. That is to say crazy families—I remember one case in which the mother, the daughter and the son—the husband they got rid of—were convinced that they were the only decent people in the world. Everybody else was dirty, couldn't cook, couldn't do anything. They were the only moral and decent ones, and they had a tremendous hate and contempt for everybody else.

Anybody who sees that thinks there is something strange about family narcissism, but what is not supposed to be strange is when we find the same phenomenon not referring to a family, but referring to the nation. The very same attitude, that my nation is the best, the most wonderful, the most this, that or the other attitude, which would sound utterly revolting or crazy is referred to the individual or family, sound praiseworthy, moral and good if it is referred to a whole national group, or a religion, for that matter.

Things are not very different psychologically with regard to group narcissism and individual narcissism. This transfer from individual narcissism to group narcissism, which has produced the phenomena of religious hatred and nationalism, is one in which not necessarily things changes in the nature of the phenomenon. But there is one thing which is important. For a poor devil who has no money, no nothing, no education, it is very difficult to uphold his individual narcissism, except if he is really, completely crazy. So for him, the shifting of individual narcissism to the nation permits him to keep the same narcissism without being crazy, because this, confirmed by everybody else, confirmed by the leaders, confirmed by the textbooks and everything allow him to assume that his nation is the most wonderful one, with a tradition and a future and justice and morality, while every other nation—especially if there are political difficulties—is a nation of worthless people of criminals, immoral, and so on.

As I emphasized before: Once one succeeds in transferring his individual narcissism to the group, one can keep the same narcissism without being crazy, because it is confirmed by everybody else. It is a general insanity the consequences of which, however, are very much the same as the consequences of individual narcissism, which I described before. You can observe, for instance, in some countries where the data are available, that usually the least educated and the poorest classes are the most narcissistic ones, are the most nationalistic ones. This certainly holds true for the United States, because many studies have shown that. Why? Because precisely there, by the very poverty of life, poverty materially and emotionally, by the very poverty of life, there is nothing the person can be proud of except his national group. And there is nothing beyond the primitive narcissism which gives him a sense of achievement, a sense of pride.

I should like to emphasize one point as a footnote. Many of you may remember what Freud once said, that Copernicus, Darwin and he wounded the narcissism of the human race very profoundly because they had shown that man is not at all the center of the universe, that he is not a special creation of God, and that even his own consciousness was of very relative significance. One might have expected, historically speaking, that therefore we would observe a great decrease in narcissism in the last two to three hundred years. But if you see the rampant nationalism which exists today, and which does not prevent people from playing with a most deadly and insane instrument, the nuclear weapon, which with a certain likelihood will lead to the destruction of the human race, then indeed you must admit, I think, that this national narcissism has still a degree of pathology and insanity which does not at all live up to the expectation of reduced narcissism in the historical process. I think we can say that while all these factors which Freud mentions have wounded severely human narcissism, they have not really destroyed it or overcome it. It seems quite clear today that we find this narcissism directed toward nationalism big government and so on, but primarily toward techniques.

Contrary and paradoxically as it sounds, it seems that also psychologically, man today is very proud of the atomic weapon, that that is what he could produce—that his capacity to destroy the world has become the object of a tremendous narcissistic focus. Or to put it differently, that the reduction of narcissism by science has not really led to a reduction of narcissism, but has led to the same narcissism being applied to the results of science in its technical form.

If we ask about the problem of mental health, the question is, how narcissism can be overcome? This in a problem with which the spiritual leaders of man have been preoccupied for several thousand years. I shall not try to fill out a program or a way in which to overcome narcissism. I should like to give, however, a theoretical consideration to one problem. You might distinguish between malignant and benign forms of narcissism.

By the *malignant form of narcissism* I mean that narcissism which you find really in the psychotic or very sick person, which is truly directed toward his own person. My appearance, my body, my thoughts my feelings, my appetite, or whatever it is, is the only real thing, the only thing that matters in the world. That is malignant because it separates me from reason, from love, from my fellow man, from everything that makes life interesting.

The *benign form of narcissism* is the one in which narcissism is not directed toward a particular area—toward my body, my thoughts, but in which it is directed toward something I accomplish, toward an achievement, toward a scientific achievement or an economic achievement or any other achievement. That is to say, I have some of this narcissistic affection, if you please, not to my own person, but to something objective which I have created. It is still narcissism, but it is benign because by creating something, at the same time—and this is a dialectical process—I also overcome some of my narcissism. I am forced to relate myself to the world in the act of producing or creating something. Then indeed, the narcissism will not lead to the naked conflict between people individually, but it will lead to a competition about the best achievement.

I am not saying that benign narcissism is the ideal, or the end of human development, but I would say it would be the next step from overcoming the personal and purely pathological narcissism which we find. And I would say that there is another way, namely if instead of a nation, the human race were to become an object of narcissism. If people could begin to be proud of the human race, rather than to feel proud of part of the human race. And it is a very strange thing how few people, in spite of the United Nations and in spite of all progress we have made in many ways have a real experience of pride in the human race. If people had the narcissistic attachment, if you please, to humanity as they have to their own children, there would be no nuclear weapon today.

All this is possible only if there in a tremendous economic and social development in each nation in the whole world. There in no way of being proud of achievement if I cannot achieve anything because I an too poor, too miserable, or if my own thought is too paralyzed by either caciquism or by bureaucracy. This way of overcoming narcissism can only occur not just by accepting certain ideas, but by fundamental change in the life of all nations of the human race which permit every human being to be proud of that which he achieves, and every nation to be proud of that which it achieves, and not of its means of destruction.

### b) Overcoming alienation

The second point I wanted to talk about is the overcoming of *alienation*. The concept of alienation has become somewhat fashionable in recent years. Let me just be very brief, saying a few words about what the concept of alienation is.

It was actually used by Hegel first, although not historically speaking precisely for the first time, but systematically for the first time. What Hegel means by alienation is the fact that I do not extend myself as a subject of my own act, as a thinking, feeling, loving person, but I extend myself and my powers in the object which I produce. That is to say, I feel myself as nothing, but I esteem myself only in the object over there which I have created, and I am in touch with myself and my own powers by being in touch with the object of my creation. In the Old Testament this is called idolatry; that is to say, man worships the work of his own hands instead of experiencing himself as the creator.

Feuerbach developed the concept of alienation with regard to religion, saying that the richer we make God, the poorer we become. Marx expressed it in a more ample way, and I quote a sentence from Marx, where he says, "The crystallization of social activity, this consolidation of what we ourselves produce into an objective power above us, going out of our control, warping our expectations, bringing to naught our calculations, is one of the chief factors in historical development up till now. . . ." [K. Marx, MEGA I, 5, p. 22. In his *Economical-philosophical Manuscripts of 1844*—MEGA I, 3, p. 130] Marx says: "The less you *are*, the less you express your life, the more you *have*. The greater is your *alienated* life, the greater is the saving of your alienated being." The impoverishment of man for the enrichment of the object he creates—that is the essence of alienation.

It is clear that the alienated man is frightened, and that he is dependent on the object—things, gadgets, commodities, bureaucracies, the state, leaders, caciques—there are many, many forms, but all have the same function of giving man a full sense of identity. Because he is in touch with himself only by surrendering to some great power, or great figure, or great institution which gives him the illusion that he is in touch with his own powers.

Alienation is not only a problem of the modern organization-man, although there is probably no period in which alienation has reached such a degree as it has reached today in Western society. But I should like to make one footnote here which has reference to the peasant—especially, I think, in Latin America; at least it is what I would observe in Mexico—and that is that one form of alienation is delivery to fate. It is expressed in the hopelessness in which the individual submits himself to fate—that there is a feeling that there is nothing he can do about life, that life has to go, has to pass as it is, and that the great problem is fate or, if you please, necessity. That you have to accept this, and if you accept it voluntarily, then you are in some way one with the greatest power there is. And that is Fate. The fatalistic lack of hope is one of the symptoms in the lack of mental health in the peasant population in Latin America. One finds a peculiar form of alienation in which fate, and alleged necessity, has become the great goddess.

If people overcome alienation, clearly this is the basis for independence, for any kind of meaningful democracy—which is more than just putting a ballot in the box. But this requires again significant social changes, namely social changes in which the individual is not submitted to caciques nor bureaucracy, in which he has a part, an active and responsible part in forming social life. It is not precisely a matter of wealth. It is not precisely a matter of conscience. It is a matter of being an active part, and that is possible only under certain conditions, one of which I believe is an optimal degree of decentralization.

### c) Overcoming necrophilia

The third concept I wanted to talk about as part of mental health is the overcoming of hostility. I should like to refer to that hostility which is a pathological factor, hostility which is not just the reaction to attacks against my life, and in that sense stands in the service of life and is generally accepted.

I distinguish between two different kinds of hostility. One I would like to call "*reactive*" hostility: hostility which is a reaction to anxiety. The frightened person is hostile provided he is so frightened and so powerless he has to repress and to suppress his hostility. But in general, if you ask what is the main source of hostility in the world, it is not the alleged evil nature in man which has become so modern today again. It is the fact that most people are frightened. I should like to say that it is a most peculiar and paradoxical phenomenon that the last four hundred years, till the end of the Middle Ages, are centuries of fright. There has never been as much security in world as today. There has never been as much insecurity as today. Insecurity both individually and emotionally, but also very realistically, because man has never lived for years in the immediate danger of all life being destroyed any moment, which he might expect or not expect.

This anxiety, which started really with the end of the Middle ages and which has existed in one form or another through the last hundreds of years, I think has come today to such a peak that rightly people like Auden and others have called our century, "The Century of Anxiety." I am not going to talk about this anxiety now, but about the fact that anxiety produces hostility and that most of the hostility you find in individuals is the hostility of frightened man. I think we live in a world of frightened men. And those who brandish the bomb are certainly not less frightened than those who are afraid of the bomb. That man is afraid today has to do with the very fact of alienation. It has to do with the very fact of the lack of social coherence, with the fact of the atomization of people, and the fact that everybody is profoundly bored with life that doesn't make much sense.

There is another type of hostility which is quite different and which I would like to call "*necrophilous*" hostility, "*malignant*" hostility. I should like to read you a definition of this which is expressed in a beautiful speech of Miguel Unamuno, which he made at the University of Salamanca in response to the speech of the Franco General, Millán Astray. General Millán had a motto which you find in many fascists, consciously and explicitly, and in many today, not so consciously and not so explicitly, namely the motto, "Long Live Death." After his speech, Miguel Unamuno got up and said, "Just now I have heard a necrophilous and senseless cry, 'Long Live Death.'" I want to call your attention to the word "necrophilous". You know necrophilia is a perversion which denotes the desire of a man to have intercourse with the body of a dead woman. Well, that is rare, but it exists. Unamuno here uses it in a much wider sense, namely the love for death, the attraction to death.

And Unamuno went on saying: "I who have spent my life shaping paradoxes which have aroused the uncomprehending anger of others, I must tell you on expert authority that this outlandish paradox is repellent to me. General Millán is a cripple. Let this be said without any slighting undertones. He is a war invalid. So was Cervantes. Unfortunately there are all too many cripples in Spain who have such views. And soon there will be even more of them if God does not come to our aid. It pains me to think that General Millán should dictate the patterns of mob psychology. The cripple who lacks the spiritual greatness of a Cervantes is wont to seek ominous release in causing mutilation around him. This is a temple of the intellect, a university, and I am its High Priest. It is you who profane its sacred precincts. You will win because you have more than enough full troops. But you will not convince. For to convince, you need to persuade and in order to persuade you would need what you lack, reason and right in the struggle. I consider it futile to exhort you to think of Spain. I have done." [Cited according to H. Thomas, 1961, p. 354f.]

Unamuno saw very clearly the essence of this attitude to love death. It is a necrophilic attitude. It is an attitude in which death, destruction, decay have a perverse attraction. I would say that this perhaps is the only true perversion that exists, namely to be attracted by death while one is alive. And you find this necrophilous attitude in a minority of people. They are the ones who are able to persuade the many who are furious and angry because they are frightened. The furious and angry ones you can change easily, because all you need to do is to remove their fright. Well, that's not easy, because in order to remove their fright, you must make their lives meaningful. But you will not change easily the necrophile. It is very important to recognize them—and to recognize them as the worst aberration of human sanity that exists.

One of the most blatant examples of this necrophilic hostility was Hitler. There is a story of Hitler which is not authenticized but very likely. In the First World War, another soldier found Hitler in a trance, looking at the decayed corpse of another soldiers and it was very difficult to get him away and to get him out of this trance. This was the same man who persuaded himself and who persuaded millions of people that his aim was the improvement and salvation of the people. And yet, in his last days it was clear that his real aim was the destruction of everything. And the real fulfilment of a character like Hitler's, of the truly necrophilic character, is total destruction, and not life.

I know that one would have to talk a great deal more about it to make this concept more understandable. I should like to mention in passing that what Freud has described as the anal character is the more frequent and malignant form of what in its malignant form is the necrophilous character. The anal character is attracted only to faeces and dirt, but when it changes into its more malignant form, attracted to death and all that is in contrast to life.

This capacity for the attraction to death is one which is given in any human being if he fails in development of what I would call his primary potentiality, namely to be related to life as something which in interesting, something which is joyful, or to develop his powers of love and reason. If all of these things remain incomplete, then man is prone to develop another form of relatedness, that of destroying life. By doing this he also transcends life, because it is as much of a transcendence to destroy life as to create it.

To be able to create life, and by that I don't mean to create children, but the creation of all that is alive—we need certain individual and social conditions. But even the most unhappy and impoverished man can destroy, and in destroying he gets even with his own what Unamuno calls his crippledness. You might say, necrophilous destructiveness is the transcendence of the cripple, a perverse creation of the cripple in which he destroys because he cannot create.

Again, if in the long run, this necrophilous destructiveness is to be diminished, the solution clearly lies in life conditions which permit man to unfold individually with faith in himself, where he can reasonable be dependent on another person, but without feeding from him, not eating him up. The positive expression is that of what I have called the *productive orientation* of the independent and free man.

## d) Social determinants of mental health

Let me say a few words on the historical conditions, in which man functions as a reflex of the society in which he lives and—interestingly enough—not only of the present but also of the past. If we could take an x-ray of any individual in any given society, you would find the history of—the social history of the last five hundred years at least in that individual. You only would have to make it explicit. Most of these things, these attitudes, are the result of the history of this group to which he belongs. And you might say you find also in the individual a future that has not been realized as yet. You will find that societies have a future, even though they have not achieved it yet, but who are marching toward the future, and they will show in the individual in a phase of need for capacity and energy. This characterizes every individual in the same society. And even if they are not yet decayed, even if they might still be at the height of their strength, show already in the individual features which are indications of the future.

The individual is precisely the frozen expression of the past and even of the future. And hence, mental health in any sense can be conceived only in terms of what is the aim, what is the goal, what is society marching toward, and where it is coming from. Of all symptoms of the lack of mental health, there is one which seems to me the worst one: the lack of hope. This is one of the roots of all the disease symptoms, whether it's alcoholism or homicide or lack of discipline or corruption. You find it where there is little hope. What I am saying is only paraphrasing something Goethe once said, "There is no greater distinction between historical figures than that between those who have belief and those who lack belief." Those who believe are alive, and those lack belief are dead. And what holds true for the society holds true for the individual living in that society.

Mental health would be a syndrome of unalienated, relatively not narcissistic, not anxious and not destructive, but productive individuals. If I could give it a very general expression: people who are interested in life. That is true for any individual. And obviously, the capacity to be interested in life depends not only on individual factors, but on very significant social factors. The main form of coping with mental illness and trying to achieve mental health, is not primarily individual therapy, but is primarily the change of those social conditions which produce mental illness or lack of mental health in the various forms which I have tried to describe.

# III. The Humanistic Science of Man

# PRELIMINARY CONSIDERATIONS

Our present epoch is characterized by the discrepancy that exists between our scientific and technical knowledge on the one hand, and the little knowledge we as yet have about man, on the other.

This is not just a theoretical discrepancy, but a most important practical one as well: if man cannot know more about himself, and use this knowledge for the better organization of his life, he will be destroyed by the very products of his scientific knowledge. But isn't this need for man to gain a better knowledge of himself not already being met by the thousands of investigators in the fields of psychology, social psychology, psychoanalysis, human relations, etc.? The answer to this question is vital with regard to the foundation of a new "institute for the science of man." If one feels that the aims of a science of man are being adequately covered by the existing social sciences, then indeed one should be strengthening the existing framework and not be founding new institutes.

Those participating in the discussions about the new Institute very clearly hold that the existing social sciences do not provide what is needed.

These are some of the reasons for this conviction:

(1) The social sciences of today (with a number of notable exceptions), impressed by the success and prestige of the natural sciences, try to apply the methods of the natural sciences to the furthering of man. Not only do they not ask themselves whether the method valid for the study of things is also valid for the study of man, but they even fail to question whether this concept of the scientific method is not naive and outdated. They believe that only a method which counts and weighs can be called scientific, forgetting that the most advanced natural sciences today, such as theoretical physics, operate with bold hypotheses based on imaginative inferences. Even intuition, according to Einstein, should not be despised. The result of this imitation of a badly understood scientific method is that the method of "facts and figures" determines the problems one studies. Researchers choose insignificant problems because the answers can be put into figures and mathematical formulae, instead of choosing significant problems and developing new methods suitable to the study of these problems.

The result is that there are thousands of research projects, most of which do not touch on the fundamental questions of man. The thinking applied in these projects is not rigorous but rather of a naive, practical-technical nature, and it is no wonder that the advanced natural sciences rather than the social sciences attract the best brains of the nation.

(2) Closely related to the problem of a misunderstood scientific method is the relativism with which the social sciences are imbued. While we still pay lip service to the great humanistic tradition, most social scientists have adopted an attitude of complete relativism, an attitude in which values are considered a matter of taste but of no objective validity. Because it is a difficult task to probe the objective validity of values, social science has chosen the easier path of throwing them out altogether. In

doing so, it has neglected the fact that our whole world is endangered by the increasing loss of a sense of values, which has led to an increasing incapacity to use constructively the fruits of our thoughts and efforts in the natural sciences.

(3) Another aspect of this relativism is the loss of a concept of man as a definite entity underlying the various manifestations of man as they appear in various cultures. One studies man as if he were a blank sheet of paper on which every culture writes its own text, rather than as a being that is not only biologically but also psychologically a definable entity. If we do not regain this concept of man as an underlying reality, how can we expect to make fruitful use of the growing geographical and social unity of man, which is the historical trend of the future?

# GENERAL AIMS

In the light of these preliminary considerations, we arrive at the formulation of the general aim of the Institute, which is to pursue the scientific study of man in the spirit of humanism. More specifically, this has the following implications. Firstly, the study of man must be based on certain humane concerns, primarily those which have been the concern of the whole humanistic religious and philosophical tradition: the idea of the dignity of man and of his potentialities for love and reason which can be actualized under favorable circumstances. Secondly, the study of man must be based on those concerns which result from our own historical situation: the breakdown of our traditional value system, the uncontrolled and unstructured growth of purely intellectual and technical activities, and the resulting need to find a new, rational foundation for the establishment of the values of the humanistic tradition. These concerns assume that in spite of all differences man is one species, not only biologically and physiologically but also mentally and psychologically.

These general aims can be accomplished only if methods proper to the study of man are examined and developed. The problem is not that of choosing between a scientific and a non-scientific study of man, but of determining what constitutes the proper rational method for the understanding of man and what does not.

A humanistic science of man must continue the work of the great students of man of the past, such as Aristotle and Spinoza. It will be enriched by the new data which biology, physiology and sociology are giving us, and by our own experiences as contemporaries in this age of transition who are concerned with the future of man.

In this latter respect one more remark appears to be necessary. It is often said by social scientists that one condition of scientific inquiry is the absence of any self-interested or preconceived aims. That this is a naive assumption is clearly shown by the development of the natural sciences: they are to a large extent furthered and not hindered by practical aims and necessities. It is the task of the scientist to keep his data objective, not to study without aims—which are what give meaning and impulse to his work. Just as every age has its specific economic and technical problems, so it also has its specific human problems, and the study of man today must be prompted and guided by the problems engendered in this period of world history.

# SPECIFIC AIMS

(1) *The study of the methods proper for the science of man:* It has to be established what differences in approach exist between the study of things and the study of living beings, especially man. For instance, there is a difference between the "objective" approach, in which the "object" is nothing but an object, and an approach in which the observer at the same time relates empathically to the persons he observes.

(2) *The study of the concept of man and of human nature:* While humanistic philosophy assumes the unity of all mankind, there is a great need for rational and demonstrable proof that there is indeed such a thing as man and human nature beyond the purely anatomical and physiological realm. The concept of human nature must be established by integrating what we know of man in the past with what we know of man in various highly developed and relatively primitive cultures today. The task is to go beyond a descriptive anthropology, and to study the basic human forces behind the manifold varieties in which it is expressed. The thoroughgoing dynamic study of all manifestations of human nature will lead to the inference of a tentative picture of human nature and what the laws governing it

are. A humanistic science of man must begin with the concept of human nature, while at the same time aiming to discover what this human nature is. Needless to say, a number of studies should be made of different societies (industrial, preindustrial, primitive) in which hypotheses on human nature should be tested.

(3) *The study of values:* It must be shown that certain values are not simply matters of taste, but are rooted in the very existence of man. It has to be demonstrated which these such basic values are and how they are rooted in the very nature of man. Values in all cultures must be studied in order to find any underlying unity; and a study of the moral evolution of mankind must also be attempted. Furthermore, it is necessary to investigate what effect the violation of basic ethical norms has on the individual and on the culture. According to the relativists, any norm is valid once it is established by the culture whether it is murder or love. Humanism claims that certain norms are inherent in man's existential situation, and that their violation results in certain consequences which are inimical to life.

(4) *The study of destructiveness:* Related to the above is the study of destructiveness in all its forms: destruction of others, self-destruction, sadism, and masochism. We know almost nothing about the causes of destructiveness, and yet there is an enormous field of empirical data which would permit us to establish at least hypotheses concerning the individual and social causes of destructiveness.

(5) *The study of creativeness:* There is an equally broad field of observation for the study of creative impulses in children, adolescents and adults, as well as of the factors which further or

impede these impulses. The study of creativeness, as of destructiveness, must transcend the American scene and, if possible, use material from as many diverse cultures as can be obtained.

(6) *The study of authority:* The modern age of freedom and individualism has fought against authority and established as its ideal the complete absence of authority. This absence of overt authority, however, has helped to increase the power of anonymous authority, which, in turn, has led to a dangerous degree of conformity. It is necessary to study the problem of authority afresh and to differentiate empirically between irrational and rational forms of authority; also to study the phenomenon of conformism in all its manifestations.

(7) *Study of the psychological premises of democratic organization:* The idea of the responsible and well informed citizen who participates in the important decisions of the community is the central concept of democracy. But due to the quantitative increase in population and to the influence of methods of mass suggestion, the substance of democracy is weakening. Studies are necessary to show what goes on in the mind of the voter (beyond polling his opinion), how suggestible he is, what the fact that he can do little to influence political action does to the alertness of his political thinking. Experiments in group discussion and decision-making must be furthered, and their results studied.

(8) *Study of the educational process:* The fact is that we have more higher education than any people ever had anywhere in the world, but that our system of higher education does relatively little to stimulate critical thought and to influence character formation. As a number of studies have shown, the

students are little affected by their teachers' personalities and, at best, get not much more than purely intellectual knowledge. New studies are needed to examine the learning situation and the student-teacher relationship. How can education can go beyond purely verbal intellectual processes into the realm of meaningful experience?

(9) *Study of history as the evolution of man:* Conventional history was studied in a provincial way. The roots of our culture in Palestine, Greece and Rome, and then European and American history, were in the center of attention. We need a true world history in which the evolution of man is shown in its right proportions. It must be shown how the same basic ideas have arisen in various branches of the human family, how some have merged and others remained separate, although the differences have been greatly overstated in comparison to the similarities. In a true History of Man, the evolution of man, his character and his ideas could be shown as well as his growth into an ever more integrated unity. Due emphasis would be given to the true proportions of various cultures and ages. Such a history should enable man to have an objective picture of the whole human race, its growth, integration, and unity. In recent years a number of universal histories more or less answering to this type have been written, but they do not meet the real need, which is that for a scholarly work of many volumes, written by a number of outstanding specialists united by a humanistic spirit.

# GENERAL REMARKS

(1) The Institute, in order to have any value, must have a distinctive image. This image cannot be adequately expressed in words (not so much because we have no words, but because they are misused in double-talk) but must rather be expressed by people who in their work and personalities express this image.

(2) The Institute should not follow the practice of the big foundations which has been in practice to encourage many people to think about a scientific problem in terms of what they can "sell" to a foundation, to think first about the funding and only later about what one wants to discover. The Institute should make money available only to the extent that a project really needs it. As a matter of principle, budgets should be kept within a reasonable minimum and should be entirely functional. In this way, the Institute would try to encourage the return to an old-fashioned way of working in which thinking and studying, and not the obtaining of funds and their administration, are at the center of research.

(3) The Institute should support two kinds of activities (as well as building up a library devoted to the science of man):

(a) The work of outstanding scholars: here the goal should not be a specific problem, but rather to support a productive personality who should be enabled to pursue his research into the science of man free from other restricting obligations.

(b) Specific research problems to be tackled by gifted people. The discovery of such persons could be one of the tasks of the Institute. Here grants should be given for specific projects.

The governing body of the Institute should develop its own research policy, not only choosing gifted people but also problems on the basis of an integrated study of the whole field. The governing body of the Institute would be, to an extent, a scientific planning body for the study of man.

(4) The Institute should support people and projects outside as well as inside of the U.S.A. Under no circumstances should grants be given to universities or other such bodies. Only persons and specific projects suggested and accepted by the Institute should receive grants.

(5) It is suggested that the Institute has an active governing body of 5–7 members who meet for at least a whole week twice a year, in order to discuss not only grants but the general plans for work, and to devote some time during the year to the preparation of this work in their own field. Such a body

should be composed of representatives of various branches in the field of the science of man, but members should primarily be chosen on the basis of common principles, productivity and individual imagination. The bureaucratic spirit should be kept to a minimum.

# IV. Is Man Lazy by Nature?

# 1. THE AXIOM OF MAN'S INHERITED LAZINESS

## a) Socio-economic aspects of the axiom

Nobody can escape the influence of an axiom we all are taught from childhood on, that of man's innate laziness. This axiom does not stand by itself. It is part of the more general assumption, that man is evil by nature and hence needs the Church or the power of the state to try to extirpate the evil even though he can never hope to succeed in this attempt beyond a certain measure. If—so the argument runs—man is lazy, greedy, destructive by nature, he needs rulers—spiritual and secular—who restrain him from following his inclinations.

But it is historically more correct to reverse the sequence: if institutions and leaders want to rule men, their most efficient ideological weapon is to convince him that he cannot be trusted to follow his own will and insight, because both are guided by the devil within him. As nobody has seen more clearly than Nietzsche, if one succeeds in filling man with the permanent feeling of sin and guilt, he will be incapable of being free, of being himself, because his self is corrupted and hence must not be permitted to assert itself. Man can react to this fundamental accusation with abject submission, or protest against it—and thus seemingly prove it—with violent aggression, but he cannot be free, he cannot be the master of his own life; he cannot be himself.

Before entering into the examination of the question itself we do well to consider another consequence, aside from the one just mentioned, of the answer. If man is lazy by nature, indolent and passive, then he is motivated to be active only by stimuli which are not *intrinsic* to the activity itself, but *extrinsic* to it; essentially by reward (pleasure) and punishment (pain).

If man is lazy by nature, the question is, what incentives are necessary to overcome this innate inertia? If man is active by nature, the question is, what are the circumstances that paralyze man's natural aliveness and make him lazy and uninterested.

This idea that man is lazy by nature and that his activity had to be stimulated by extrinsic stimuli has been, as we all know, the basis of the generally accepted notions about *education* and work. The pupil had to be made to learn by all kinds of rewards or punishments. It is only relatively recently (for instance Friedrich Wilhelm Fröbel or Maria Montessori) that one began to see that the child wanted to learn, if the learning process itself was interesting. But this view is still not generally accepted and the main efforts in education were made in the direction of finding better extrinsic stimuli rather than discovering methods of teaching that stimulate the pupils' natural wish to learn, to know and to discover. One cannot even say that the belief in the sole efficacy of rewards and punishment is an old-fashioned one. Behaviorism, especially in its latest and most sophisticated form of Skinner's neo-behaviorism, has made the principle of the exclusive efficacy of extrinsic compensation the cornerstone of his whole system.

Only the insight that well timed rewarding is more effective than punishment constitutes the advance over the older views.

That industrial society has adopted the same principle with regard to *work* hardly needs to be demonstrated. That work, especially of the industrial worker was disagreeable and unpleasant nobody I doubted a hundred years ago, because it was so obvious. Its duration (up to 14 or even 16 hours a day), its physical discomfort and the need to expend a great deal of physical energy in unhealthy environments, made it very definitely repulsive. Today much has changed: the working time is greatly reduced, machines replace human energy, the place of work is not dark and unhealthy any more; moreover what is left of "dirty work" is mainly done by the lowest strata of the population, in U.S.A. by black workers, in Europe by Italian, Spanish, Turkish "Guest workers"—and women.

Today one unpleasant aspect of work has become conspicuous, after the more visible negative aspects have been greatly diminished: the *boredom* that is inherent in the work not only of blue collar workers, but of employees and bureaucrats, with the exception of those who participate in planning and decision making.

But whether it is physical discomfort or the psychical discomfort of boredom, both sides, workers and employers, agreed that work was by necessity unpleasant, and that in order to motivate the worker to work at all he needed to be threatened with starvation, and in order to make him work better and more productively one needed to reward him by higher wages and a shorter working day. However, although both sides agreed on the principle, the employers were reluctant to raise wages and often had to be "motivated" by the capacity of the workers to strike. Simultaneously the fundamental changes in the economic system made it also advantageous for the employers to increase the rewards. Inasmuch as there were conflicts between workers and bosses, they were centered around wages and length of the working day. That the quality of the working process could be changed in such a way that work itself could become interesting, was hardly thought of by either side.

It is a remarkable phenomenon that this was so, at least on the side of the workers, in spite of the fact that Marx, so influential in many other respects, had recognized that the crucial problem is that of the *nature of work*. The work of the worker or employee in capitalism, is, according to Marx, alienated work. The worker sells his energy to the one who hires him, does what he is told to do, as if he were part of a machine; the commodity "he" manufactures stands over and against him, he does not experience himself as its creator. Alienated work is necessarily boring and hence painful and uncomfortable; as a consequence the worker can be motivated to accept the pain of work because he is rewarded by material compensations, consisting essentially in increased consumption. Conflicts do not arise over the principle but only over the size of the compensation.

The situation would be entirely different if work would not be alienated, i.e. if it is intrinsically rewarding because it is interesting, stimulating, enlivening, and if not the work itself in a narrower sense, the responsible participation in the working unit (plant, hospital, etc.) as a social organization.

It is only in recent years that the workers have taken up Marx's point, although certainly not by the direct influence of his writings. This new attitude is very visible in the U.S. and in the German Federal Republic. For some years already the complaint about the boredom of work and the demand for methods of production that give the worker the possibility of greater interest, influence of the work process, decentralization of the overspecialized work process have become central issues in negotiations between workers and employers, even though purely economic demands for higher wages (or at least stable wages in terms of their purchasing power) are still of equal importance. From the side of industry these demands for more satisfactory work have found some understanding, and some attempts in this direction have been made, at least in an experimental and tentative way.

The crucial importance of the question for the future should be obvious. To the degree to which work is more mechanized, impersonal and hence alienated, the greater must be the extrinsic reward: This reward consists in higher wages, that is to say more consumption. This leads to the development in which modern man must find his mental balance by ever increasing consumption as compensation for the ever increasing boredom of work, and of leisure.

If one is aware of the dangerous human deterioration which consumerism brings about, the question whether it is true that man is lazy by nature is one of the most important psychological-anthropological questions that can be raised.

### b) Scientific aspects of the axiom

It is difficult to understand how one could have so firmly believed in the idea of the natural laziness and passivity of man in view of the fact that so many observations point to the contrary. Did not animals show an irresistible tendency to play? Were not children eager to play, and were they not active until they became tired? (That Freud should have misunderstood the tendency of a child to repeat the same game again and again as an expression of a "repetition compulsion" rather than as an expression of the need for activity is probably due to the axiom of natural inertia.) Does not man in all ages and cultures show a need for excitation and stimulation? Does he not seek it in art, drama, literature, ritual, dance, and in our culture by watching "the man on the flying trapeze," automobile accidents, reading about crimes, illness; does he not do everything he can to avoid boredom and inertia?

According to the reductionist axiom man seeks for a state of minimal excitation. For Freud pleasure consists in the very absence of excitation. Wouldn't be boredom and inertia ideal states? Why man seeks to avoid these states? There is ample evidence for man's inherent need for excitement and stimulation, and it will be discussed shortly: what I want to say at this point is only that even the unsifted first-hand evidence of everyday observation demands an explanation for the blindness of most psychologists to the fact of the inherent need for excitement and stimulation.

D. O. Hebb offers one very ingenious explanation for this puzzling phenomenon. He suggests that much of the current trouble with motivation theory lies in the fact that psychologists have based their thinking on dated neurological theories which in the meantime have been replaced by more adequate ones. "Characterologically," remarks Hebb (1955, p. 244), "stimulus-response theory has treated the animal as more or less inactive unless subjected to special conditions of arousal. These conditions are first, hunger, pain and sexual excitement; and secondly, stimulation that has become associated with one of these more primitive motivations." Pre-1930 neurology, as Hebb points out, tended to believe that the nerve cell is inert until something happens to it from the outside, and the same would be true of the collection of cells that make up the nervous system. Since 1930 neurology has changed considerably in this respect. One began to recognize that the nervous system like all living things is active, that the human brain is built to be active, and that all it needs is adequate nutrition; that, as Hebb points out, *the only behavioral problem is to account for inactivity, not for activity.* (Ibid.) Recent neurological findings show that the brain is always active, but that its "activity is not always the transmitted kind that conduces to behavior." (Ibid., p. 248; Hebb quotes as evidence the distinction between the slow-burning activity of the dendrites and the firing activity indicated in the *spikes.*)

Impressive as Hebb's statement is, that psychologists theories suffer from the fact that they are based on a dated neurological theory, it fails to answer the question why psychologists have not used a more up-to-date neurology. Why should they have disregarded data which were at hand and ready to be used?

### c) Work and the axiom of man's innate passivity

Perhaps the main reason for the faith in the axiom of man's innate passivity lies in the very nature of work in the industrial society. This becomes very clear if we compare industrial work—from manufacturing at the mechanical loom to the conveyor belt to the assembly line in an automobile plant—with the work of the medieval artisan. The smith or the carpenter worked in a way that required their constant concentration and interest in the work. This work was a continuous learning process, starting with apprenticeship, continuing throughout the entire life of the artisan. In the process of working, he increased his skill, i.e., *he developed himself*, his senses, his knowledge of the material, of the techniques; his ability to sense, to see, increased throughout his life. He grew in the process of this kind of activity based on his relatedness to his materials, his tools, and many other factors in his environment. Hence this work was never boring, but interesting, like any activity requiring concentration, attention and the practice of a skill.

Today we see still remnants of this older attitude toward work in the artist (from the same root as 'artisan') be he a painter or a cellist, in the work of a surgeon, a fisherman, a circus performer, etc. (This seems to be the reason why people today are fascinated by watching any skilled work process which they have the occasion to see—the playing of Casals, as well as watching a weaver at work.)

In fact, we know that in work requiring constant exercise and practice, skills develop which seem miraculous to the outsider. Shepherds whose eyesight is ten times that of the average man today; Arab carpenters who could by sight and touch and without the use of measuring instruments prepare a slab of marble that fitted exactly into the space left for it in a table (I am indebted for these examples to personal communications with the painter Max Hunziker); the violinist who can play a large number of complex musical pieces by ear could not develop these extraordinary faculties other than by constant activity and practice, even though talent will be an element in the quality of their performance. The examples must suffice to remind the reader of this kind of work.

This kind of skilled work does not require extrinsic rewards or threats of punishment to be performed. It carries with it the intrinsic reward of interest, the exercise of skill, relating oneself to the world by a creative act, and more than anything else, that of growing and becoming oneself.

In order to understand the nature of this kind of work one must fully understand it in its social context. The medieval artisan, like the artisan in all pre-industrialized countries today, did not aim at the maximization of profit or production. He wanted to continue his traditional standard of living, and was not obsessed by the hunger for commodities of the modern consumer. In addition, the number of apprentices he could accept as well as the amount he produced were limited by the regulations of the guilds. He would have been very surprised at the suggestion that the work he was doing was boring, and that the monetary award was the compensation for the unpleasantness of work—and the main incentive for doing it. (There is a large literature documenting this picture; cf. especially the work of Werner Sombart, Max Weber, Richard Henry Tawney, Karl Marx and also my own analysis in *Escape from Freedom* (1941a), *The Sane Society* (1955a) and *The Revolution of Hope* (1968a).

In industrial societies all this has changed. Work has only one purpose: to bring a profit to those who own the machines and to feed those who are "employed" to serve the machines. The worker today serves the machine; he requires very limited skill. Even the "skilled" worker cannot be compared with the one having the skill of an artisan. He is more like a specialized tool than like a skilled man. The unskilled worker makes a very limited number of movements; in the case of the worker on the conveyor belt, his whole body is the prisoner of the rhythm of the belt, his activity restricted to one or two monotonous movements. He is never in touch with "his" product; that is to say, not as its maker, but only as the buyer who may purchase and own it. (It is interesting in this respect that, according to a recent report Italian shipbuilding workers show a much lower degree of dissatisfaction and boredom, because their work is such that they always see their whole product—the ship—and witness its growth from the first day to its eventual birth, when it is release, into the water.) It is well known that he suffers from painful boredom and that he resents his work. He as a person is not enriched, but crippled by the working process, because none of his faculties have a chance of being practised and of growing.

This can hardly be otherwise in a system in which one produces for the sake of the profit the commodity brings, and not for its value, whether socially or culturally. One produces many commodities with built-in obsolescence, and worthless commodities which are made to appear useful only through the suggestive power of advertising and packaging. This does not mean to say, of course, that needed and valuable things are not also produced—if this were not so the economic system could not function. But profit, not usefulness or beauty is the primary purpose in capitalist production, and for this reason one cannot expect the work to have intrinsic interest.

In recent years management has begun to realize that the boredom of work is counterproductive even from the standpoint of profit, and one has begun to decentralize work again to make it less boring. The most radical attempt to change the alienated nature of work is that made in the Yugoslav system of socialism, that of self-management in which all participants of an enterprise are responsible for the management of the enterprise. The enterprise is not owned by a private owner, nor by the state (as in the Soviet bloc countries), it is not even "owned" in the strict sense of the word by the workers. Legal ownership has lost its central role because what matters is not ownership but control and participation. Even though as one would expect in a small country which is surrounded by social systems based on private or state control, the system has in practice worked only very imperfectly, it is nevertheless the most original and new idea with regard to work organization and property. (Cf. Constitution of the Socialist Federal Republic of Yugoslavia, Ch. II, Art. 6 and Ch. V, Art. 96, quoted in I. Kolaya, 1966). It is a noteworthy fact that the workers' revolutionary movements in Poland and Czechoslovakia had as their main workers' council, and there is probably no tendency which is more opposed by the Soviet Union than this trend; it had its early representatives in Germany in Rosa Luxemburg and in the beginning of the

Russian Revolution by the "workers opposition", who both were opposed to Lenin's bureaucratic methods. (Cf. for a detailed discussion of this problem E. Fromm, 1955a.)

The alienated industrial systems in the form of capitalism or so-called "socialism" are based on these premises, according to which man spends his time and energy without interest and motivated only by the wish for increasing consumption. To doubt the axiom of extrinsic incentives being man's only motivation for work means to doubt the whole system; it is putting sand in the machine that seems to function so well.

The majority of psychologists, like most social scientists, are not prone to doubt the system. In fact, their theories are not only influenced by it, but help to support it ideologically. They do not transcend the basic axioms even in their experiments, most of which tend to prove the basic premises of our society scientifically. This is all the easier since they deal little with hard data as, for instance, neurophysiologists do, and they manipulate their material—mostly of course not consciously—in the socially desirable fashion.

The very fact that in the whole academic discussion of extrinsic versus intrinsic motivation hardly any mention is made of the connection between this problem and the general assumption about motivation for work, suggests that something like a repression of this connection has taken place in order to blind the social scientist from seeing the source of his bias. (Some industrial psychologists like Lickert, McGregor, White, have made valuable contributions to the understanding of work motivation, but they are still guided by the principle of harmony between the interests of profit and the interests of the human being. Cf. E. Fromm, 1970e.)

I have tried to show that the central role of the machine, together with the organization of work as it exists in industrial society is aside from the need to make people feel guilt and hence better manipulable one reason why the axiom of man's natural laziness and his need to be activated by the extrinsic stimulation of pleasure or pain remained dominant in the thinking of most psychologists. It is a telling example for ideological influences that many neurophysiologists speak of reward and punishment areas as equivalent to pleasure and pain. It is taken for granted that even our brain follows the laws of Christian-capitalist thinking, i.e., that pleasure is a reward and pain a punishment.

But the reward principle no longer functions smoothly. The effects of boredom can be seen in numerous manifestations; in the lack of interest among many young people in working at all; in the spreading popularity of drugs; in violence; in silent or manifest despair. An increasing number of people feel that the boredom of 40 hours a week spent in working is not, and cannot be, compensated by the rewards of increasing consumption—especially when consumption itself becomes boring and is not conducive to greater activity, growth of personality and increase of skill. There is a great deal of absenteeism and psychosomatic illness among workers, and their displeasure with work shows also in the shoddiness of many products.

We find ourselves in a severe crisis of the patriarchal system centered around duty and obedience as supreme values—not life, interest, growth, activity; where to *have* and to *use* are the directing goals, and not to *be*. It is not surprising that under the impact of the social and cultural crisis, old doctrines are being questioned and people begin to wonder whether intrinsic pleasure in activity may not outweigh the extrinsic pleasure in money and consumption.

# 2. THE EVIDENCE AGAINST THE AXIOM

There is ample evidence against the axiom of man's innate laziness, most of it rediscovered within the last decades, when an increasing number of people began to doubt the old dogma that served to keep them dependent. Some of the most important sources of evidence I shall present in this chapter; it is to be found in various fields: the neurosciences, animal psychology, social psychology, child development, the learning process and in the phenomenon of dreaming.

## a) Neurophysiological Evidence

The trend to discover the intrinsic activity in the human being had its beginning with the Russian neurologist I. M. Sechenov in his *Reflexes of the Brain* published in Cambridge 1863. To the question whether the newborn child reacts passively or actively to external influences on his senses, Sechenov replied that "it is known that the first condition for the maintenance of material integrity, i.e., for the maintenance of the function of all nerves and muscles without exception, all organs must be adequately exercised: the optic nerve must be subjected to the action of light, the motor nerve must be stimulated and its muscles must contract, etc. On the other hand, we know that if the exercise of any of these organs is forcibly prevented, the person experiences a strained feeling that compels him to perform the necessary action. It is clear, therefore, that the child does not react passively to external influence." (Quoted in D. B. Lindsley, 1964.)

Even though Sechenov came to his view on the basis of belief in an innate pattern of reflexes which had to unfold and mature, it is of significance that he did come to the conclusion that newborn animals and human infants *strive* for sensory stimulation!

Much more recent investigations have gone far beyond the original assumption of Sechenov, and revolutionized popular concepts of the neuron as a static entity. New data have been found in the field of molecular neurobiology, which F. O. Schmitt considers to be "basic to brain and behavioral science." (F. O. Schmitt, 1967, pp. 209–219. Schmitt quotes as the definite papers on this subject those by M. V. Edds on "Neuronal Specificity and Neurogenesis," J. D. Ebert on "Molecular and Cellular Interactions in Development," and by L. Levine on "Immunochemical Approaches to the Study of the Nervous System"—all in the same volume.) "The living neuron" Schmitt (l. c., p. 211) writes, "thus differs markedly from the static entity likely to be inferred from anatomic textbooks or from the observations of physiologists whose primary concern is with bioelectric parameters. *Dynamism is the leitmotiv of neuronal function.*"

The nervous cells show a remarkable degree of activity, as well as integration. In contrast to assumptions underlying the stimulus-response psychology, "the brain is not merely *reactive* to outside stimuli, it is itself spontaneously *active.*" (R. B.

Livingston, p. 501). Livingston expresses his critique of the conventional S-R concepts in the following paragraph. "When we analyze the learning paradigm, for example, we tend to emphasize stimulus leading to response (S-R). We are inclined by this schema to fix our attention on the evoked nature of the process, on the conditional stimulus (CS), and the unconditional stimulus (UCS) which, when applied appropriately, yield a conditional response (CR). We must remind ourselves that these processes occur within a larger framework. Certain conditions are prerequisite before any stimuli can lead to learning. A stimulus (CS or UCS) becomes important only when the nervous system. is properly oriented and appropriately receptive toward the stimulus" (l. c., p. 501).

Spontaneous electrical activity of brain cells begins in embryonic life and never ceases. It can be detected by means of electrodes implanted into various regions of the brain. The amazing degree of brain cell activity can be inferred from the fact that the human brain, although it comprises only two percent of the body weight, consumes 20% of the body's oxygen at rate. This rate compares to the amount consumed by an active muscle; but while an "active muscle can sustain such a rate of oxygen consumption for only a short period . . . the nervous system continues its high rate for a lifetime, awake or asleep from before birth until death." (R. B. Livingston, l. c. p. 501. The author refers to S. S. Ketty, 1957.)

A crucial fact for the understanding of human behavior is that of the connection between brain activity, i.e., use of the neurons, and their *growth*. The development of the brain before and during a few months after birth is a very rapid one. Following this period of explosive growth (from about 335 grams at birth to 1300 grams at adulthood, the rate of acceleration decreases. The development of the brain in adult life is essentially not one of volume but one of the macromolecular structure, particularly the growth in the size of the nerve prolongations, and hence also in the weight of the neurons. After differentiation neurons rarely divide (with the exception of microneurons. Yet there is no point beyond in which this development ceases. (Cf. F. O. Schmitt, 1967, p. 211.) This neural growth occurs not only in the nerve cells within the brain, but also *in vitro*, where nerve cells in a tissue culture continue to be biologically and electrically active, and "show nuclear rotation, protoplasmic movements, axonal flow and marvellously dynamic growth cones." (R. B. Livingston, l. c. p. 502. He refers to C. M. Pomerat, 1964.)

Assumptions made in interneuronal theories of memory support the idea that the transmission of new information to the brain leads to the formation of new neural circuits which have been attributed to the shrinking or swelling of nerve processes as a result of use or disuse. Since the interneural theory has been in disrepute in the last decades, these assumptions may also be questionable. (Cf. J. Altman, 1967, p. 725.) But impressive animal experiments seem to confirm the connection between use of the neurons and their growth. In a series of experiments (cf. E. L. Bennet et al., 1964, quoted by J. Altman, l. c. p. 741) with rats the animals were divided in "enriched" ones, which were raised in a larger cage where they could move about freely and play with various objects, and in "restricted" ones reared in small isolation cages and thus deprived of both sensory stimulation and the opportunity for motor exercise. The investigators found that the cortical gray matter was thicker in the "enriched" animals (although their body weight tended to be lower), than in the "restricted" animals. J. Altman and G. D. Das (1964), in a comparable study investigated the affection cellular proliferation in the brains of rats reared in enriched and restricted environments. They obtained histological evidence of an increase in the area of the cortex in the enriched animals, and autoradiographic evidence of an enhanced rate of cellular proliferation with mature enriched animals. While further work was going on, Altman (1967, p. 741) reports as a preliminary result that other behavioral variables, such as "handling rats during infancy," can radically alter the development of the brain, in particular cell proliferation in such structures as the cerebelar cortex, the hoppocampal dentate gyrus, and the neocortex.

Other experiments which point in a similar direction are those made by T. N. Wiesel and D. H. Hubel (1965 and 1965a). These experiments show that non-use of an eye for three months after birth (by artificial lid closure) results in blindness in the deprived eye of the kitten, and that use of the eye from 3 to 15 months showed only slight visual recovery. E. R. Kandel (1967, p. 684) conclude: "Although it is only possible to produce these alterations in newborn animals the interesting possibility exists that qualitatively similar although more subtle changes in synaptic efficacy might also occur in adult animals following prolonged periods of altered usage. At present there is little understanding of the manipulations that produce permanent changes in adult animals following prolonged periods of altered usage." (Cf. also the work of F. B. Beswick and R. T. W. L. Conroy, 1965.)

Even though the present knowledge about the connection between use and growth of brain cells is very limited, certain observations about the process of aging can be of interest. W. Grey Walter (1957) writes: "The brain is not in general a limiting factor for the duration of life. The EEG changes little with the passing of the years; leaving aside the cases of authentic senility, it frequently shows the same feature at the age of 60 or at 80. Gerontology . . . has obtained from electrophysiology only the conviction that most brains can survive the rest of the organs."

Another neurophysiological phenomenon seems to point to the fact of the brain's need for activation: that of the so called pleasure areas in the brain. (The main work on this subject has been done by M. E. Olds and J. Olds, R. G. Heath and C. M. R. Delgado. Cf. especially R. G. Heath (Ed.), 1964.). The pleasure areas were discovered, first by Olds and then studied by Delgado, Heath and others; these investigators showed that if one briefly stimulates electrically certain parts of the subcortical area of the brain, a sensation of pleasure is aroused in the subject. The areas of the brain thus far found to have such apparent properties are the head of the caudate nucleus, the septal area, the amygdala, the central median thalamus, the mid-hypothalamus, the posterior hypothalamus and the boundary between the hypothalamus and the tegmentum. By placing electrodes in these various areas of the brain they could be stimulated and, conversely, the electric activity of each area could be noted on an electroencephalogram (EEG), connected with theses areas. R. G. Heath (1964, p. 79) notes that "the range of rewarding currents appeared to be significantly wider" when the septal area was stimulated, although he cautions that "too few electrode sites have been carefully explored to provide definite evidence on this point."

In a later paper R. G. Heath (1964a, p. 239) reports that "a pleasurable response was associated with focal activation of the septal region" and "that physiologic activity in the septal region is basic to the pleasure response." He also reports that non-schizophrenic patients experience more intense pleasure reactions to stimulation of the brain than schizophrenic patients which "also seems noteworthy in view of the history of 'anhedonia' (lack of pleasure) in the schizophrenic patient." He reports furthermore that sexual arousal was induced in other patients with stimulation of the septal region, but not with stimulation of other regions.

C. M. R. Delgado in a report in *Psychology Today* (1970) estimates that while 60% of the brain is neutral as far as pleasure or pain are concerned, 35% can arouse pleasure and only 5% pain. The relevance of these findings for the appreciation of Freud's theory of pleasure is evident. Freud, as well as other reductionists, believed. that there is no pleasure as such but only different degrees of pain, and that pleasure was essentially the transition from a higher to a lesser degree of pain. The neurophysiologic findings just mentioned show that pleasure has its own neurophysiological basis, and furthermore, that the human organism is "by nature" much more prepared to experience pleasure than to experience pain.

The crucial question, however, is what is meant by "pleasure." Is it primarily the satisfaction of certain physiological needs like sexual needs and hunger ("higher" pleasures being sublimations of lower ones, as in Freud's scheme), or is pleasure a general state of wellbeing beyond that of the satisfaction of specific appetites? The investigations of R. G. Heath show that stimulation of the septal region can produce sexual arousal, or in the reverse that sexual arousal appears in the EEG as being connected with the septal region. But Heath has taken an important step forward by observations that seem to transcend the hedonistic scheme altogether. I am referring to his finding that electrical stimulation of the septal area can result in an experience of *active interest*, such as for instance intellectual or other kinds of interest not related to the satisfaction of appetites like sex and hunger. He quotes one instance where in the process of solving an interesting mathematical problem, activity of the septal region was found in the EEG and he believes that it is likely that the activation of the pleasure area can result from the process of taking an active interest in the world outside (in my own terminology this would be a productive interest rather than a passive-receptive one). In other words, his discoveries point to the fact that man's active interest in the world outside is grounded in the very structure of the brain, and hence does not need to be fostered by extrinsic rewards. If man is lacking this active interest he is sick, he suffers indeed from a severe sickness which, however, Heath does not consider as a psychotic depression.

The important conclusion from these findings is that the person incapable of seeking for pleasure and—on a higher level of personality—of being actively interested in people, things, ideas, is *sick*, not as the axiom says "normally" inert.

Aside from the neurophysiological evidence that speaks against the axioms of man's innate passivity there are other data pointing to the same conclusion from experiments in animal, social and individual psychology.

### b) Evidence by experiments in animals

Among the students of animal behavior there are some who have arrived at the anti-reductionistic position on the basis of direct observation and experiments. Harry F. Harlow, Margaret K. Harlow and Donald R. Meyer (1950) contrary to the general belief that rewards and fear of punishment are the most important motivations for behavior, discovered in their experiments with monkeys that these are more motivated by the pleasure of solving a difficult task than by extrinsic rewards. They found that "monkeys would learn to unassemble a three-device puzzle with no other 'drive' and no other 'reward' than the privilege of un-assembling it." (Quoted from J. McV. Hunt, 1963, p. 40.)

In another study, Harlow found that "two well-fed and well-watered monkeys worked repeatedly at un-assembling a six-device puzzle for ten continuous hours even though they were quite free of painful stimulation and quite well fed and well watered. Moreover, at the tenth hour of testing, according to Harlow, they were still 'showing enthusiasm for their work.'" (Quoted from J. McV. Hunt, l. c.) "Harlow (1950) is among the first to use the term 'intrinsic motivation' for the notion that a basis for motivation inheres within activity itself." (J. McV. Hunt, l. c., p. 42.)

Speaking of the phenomenon of man's liking for dangerous sports or frightening roller coasters, where fear is deliberately courted, or of the addiction to bridge or golf with an optimal level of frustration, or of businessmen who find it extremely difficult to retire on reaching old age, D. O. Hebb and W. R. Thompson (1954, p. 552) state: "Such behavior in man is usually accounted for as a search for prestige, but the animal data make this untenable. It seems much more likely that solving problems and running mild risks are inherently rewarding, or in more general terms, that the animal will always act so as to produce an optimal level of excitation."

D. O. Hebb and W. R. Thompson (1954) point out in the same article that animals in general seek excitement. They point to Montgomery's and Thompson's studies which show that the rat, for instance, when given the choice between familiar and unfamiliar territory will tend to the unfamiliar—the well-known exploratory drive. (Quoted in D. E. Berlyne, 1960, p. 78). A similar tendency of the rat has been shown, as the authors point out, in the McGill laboratory where rats offered two routes to food, a direct and easy one and one through a maze, will choose the difficult one in 20 to 40 per cent of the runs. The primate of whose "interest" we spoke in connection with Harlow's observation tends to be a trouble maker when things are dull. This observation, that boredom in animals creates troublesome behavior, is of immediate significance for the understanding of human aggression as I have pointed out at greater length [in *The Anatomy of Human Destructiveness*: E. Fromm, 1973a.].

Another observation pointing in the same direction is that by A. K. Myers and N. E. Miller (1954). "Well satisfied and comfortable rats will learn to press a bar or turn a wheel merely to get an opportunity to explore the opposite end of a Miller-Mowrer box." This observation is interpreted by the authors as being caused by a "boredom drive" which can be reduced under certain conditions. Also D. E. Berlyne (1960) agrees with the assumption of a "boredom drive" produced by unchanging conditions. Instead of assuming that boredom is produced by lack of stimulation, their general orientation forces these authors to assume that there is a drive for boredom; obviously in this type of thinking nothing can exist unless it is a drive!

Interesting from the point of view of the need for stimulation are the observations by one of the foremost students of primate life in the wild, Adriaan Kortlandt. He comments on the difference between chimpanzees in the zoo, and those in their natural habitat. Of the former he says that they "generally look increasingly dull and vacant with the years," while "the older wild chimpanzees seemed to be more lively, more interested in anything and more human." (A. Kortlandt, 1962, p. 131.) This quality of aliveness in the old chimpanzee in the wild is described by Kortlandt quite vividly: "Just as the chimpanzees were tolerant of the young, they deferred to the old. The grand old man of the population studied was, I should judge, over 40—considerably older than the oldest zoo chimpanzee I have ever seen. His silver-haired back was bent, his crown was gray and his face sagged. Granddad—as I called him—was evidently somewhat [physically] handicapped.... Apparently he received his, authority from his experience and the knowledge it had given him of potential dangers; more often than any of the other males, he acted as a kind of security inspector making sure that everything was safe." (A. Kortlandt, 1962, p. 131.)

It is hardly necessary to belabour the point. The zoo chimpanzee is well fed and cared for, but he lacks almost any kind of stimulation; he lives in a most limited environment, without challenge or interest; so from lack of stimulation he becomes dull and dies earlier; on the other hand, the head of the wild chimpanzees is always confronted with challenges that stimulate him, make him exercise his observation and "thinking," make him alert; hence instead of becoming dull he becomes more efficient and wise and thus remains the leader of the group. The analogy with human beings is obvious. The inmates of old-age homes who are generally as well taken care of as the chimpanzee in the zoo (sometimes perhaps less well, since they are not as valuable) have mostly the same dull expression that Kortlandt describes in the zoo chimpanzee. Quite to the contrary, an old man who as a carpenter, fisherman, scholar, teacher, goes on being stimulated and active, shows none of this dullness but, rather, aliveness and productiveness even after his physical power and even his memory have diminished.

A very different view of the effect of zoo life can be found in the work of an eminent animal observer, Heini Hediger, who was Director of the Basel Zoo. Hediger (1952, p. 46–48) claims that wild animals are as adapted ("angepasst"), in captivity as they are in freedom. He states that the cage often becomes a "new home" to be defended, and that the animal does not miss freedom because, especially those brought to the zoo at an early age, or born in captivity, has never known freedom. How many times has this argument been used in history to justify the enslavement of human beings!

### c) Evidence by social psychological experiments

The need for activity and stimulation and the negative effects of boredom were manifested convincingly in the classic socio-psychological experiment by Elton Mayo conducted at the Hawthorne Works of the Western Electric Company in Chicago, and the recent experiments on sensory deprivations. (Cf. E. Mayo, 1933 as well as F. J. Roethlisberger and W. J. Dickson, 1950. [Cf. also E. Fromm, 1955a, pp. 302–304.])

The operation selected by Mayo was that of assembling telephone coils, work which ranks as a repetitive performance, and is usually performed by women. A standard assembly bench with the appropriate equipment, and with places for five women workers was put into a room, which was separated by a partition from the main assembly room; altogether six, operatives worked in this room, five working at the bench, and one distributing parts to those engaged in the assembly. All of the women were experienced workers. Two of them dropped out within the first year, and their places were. taken by two other workers of equal skill. Altogether, the experiment lasted for five years, and was divided into various experimental periods, in which certain changes were made in the conditions of work. Without going into the details for these changes, it suffices to state that rest pauses were adopted in the morning and afternoon, refreshments offered during these rest pauses, and the working hours cut by half an hour. Throughout these changes the output of each worker rose considerably. So far, so good; nothing was more plausible than the assumption that increased rest periods and some attempt to make the worker "feel better" were the cause for increased efficiency. Many investigators might have stopped the experiment here and been satisfied to report that the various "liberal" changes made had been responsible for the increase in the productivity of labor. Mayo did not chose this procedure; he decided to see what would happen if, by arrangement with the workers the group returned to the conditions of work as they had existed in the beginning of the experiment. Rest periods, special refreshments, and other improvements were all abolished for approximately three months. To everybody's amazement this did not result in a *decrease of output* but, on the contrary, the daily and weekly output rose to a higher point than at any time before. In the next period, the old concessions were once more introduced, with the only exception that the girls provided their own food, while the company continued. to supply coffee for the midmorning snack. The output still continued to rise. And not only the output. What is equally important is the fact that the rate of absenteeism among the workers in this experiment fell by about 80 per cent in comparison with the general rate, and that a new social friendly intercourse developed among the working women participating in the experiment.

How did Mayo explain the surprising result that "the steady increase seemed to ignore the experimental changes, in its upward development?." (E. Mayo, 1933, p. 63.) If it was not the rest pauses, the tea, the shortened working time, what was it that made the workers produce more, be more healthy and more friendly among themselves? The answer is obvious: while the *technical* aspect of monotonous, uninteresting work remained, the same, and while even certain improvements like rest pauses were not decisive, the *social* aspect of the total work situation had changed, and this caused a change in the attitude of the workers. They were informed of the experiment, and of the several steps in it; their suggestions were listened to and often followed, and what is perhaps the most important point, they were aware of participating in a meaningful and interesting experiment which was important not only to themselves, but to the workers of the entire factory. While they were at first "shy and uneasy, silent and perhaps somewhat suspicious of the company's intentions," later their attitude was marked "by confidence and candour." (Ibid.) The group developed a sense of participation in the work; because they knew what they were doing, they had an aim and a purpose, and they could influence the whole procedure by their suggestions.

The results of Mayo's experiment show that even though the technical aspect of the work process remained dull and monotonous, the workers were stimulated by, and interested in the experiment, and that this relatively small amount of stimulation had far-reaching influence on their total behavior and even on their health.

A second type of experiments dealing not with increase of stimulation but with its decrease, have yielded very important empirical evidence for the thesis of man's need to be stimulated. Its importance for our problem is so great that it justifies reporting on them in quite some detail.

An early experiment by A. Karsten (1928, quoted in C. N. Cofer and M. H. Appley, 1964, p. 279) had already established the negative responses to monotonous work. The subjects were told to draw vertical lines, or to perform a similarly boring activity for as long as they could; eventually they refused to continue. The experiment by W. H. Bexton, W. Heron and T. H. Scott (1954) and those following them were much more sophisticated and interesting. The authors describe the procedure as follows: "The subjects, 22 male college students, were paid to lie on a comfortable bed in a lighted cubicle 24 hours a day, with time out for eating and going to the toilet. During the whole experimental period they wore translucent goggles which transmitted diffuse light but prevented pattern vision. Except when eating or at the toilet, the subject wore gloves and cardboard cuffs, the latter extending from below the elbow to beyond the fingertips. These permitted free joint movement but limited tactual perception. Communication between subject and experimenters was provided by a small speaker system, and was kept to a minimum. Auditory stimulation was limited by the partially sound-proof cubicle and by a U-shaped foam-rubber pillow in which the subject kept his head while in the cubicle. Moreover, the continuous hum provided by the fans, air conditioner, and the amplifier leading to earphones in the pillow produced fairly efficient masking noise."

"As might be expected from the evidence reviewed by N. Kleitman (1939) for onset of sleep following reduced stimulation in man and other animals, the subjects tended to spend the earlier part of the experimental session in sleep. Later they slept less, became bored, and appeared eager for stimulation. They would sing, whistle, talk to themselves, tap the cuffs together, or explore the cubicle with them. This boredom seemed to be partly due to deterioration in the capacity to think systematically and productively—an effect described below. The subjects also became very restless, displaying constant random movement, and they described the restlessness as unpleasant. Hence it was difficult to keep subjects for more than two or three days, despite the fact that the pay ($20 for a 24-hour day) was more than double what they could normally earn. Some subjects, in fact, left before testing could be completed." (W. H. Bexton, W. Heron and T. H. Scott, 1954, p. 71.)

The general effect of the relative sensory deprivation was, in addition to what I mentioned already, "unusual emotional lability" during the experimental period. After the experiment the subjects reported "feelings of confusion, headaches, a mild nausea and fatigue; these conditions persisted in some cases for 24 hours after the session." (l. c., p. 72.)

The authors were primarily concerned with cognitive disturbances during the period of isolation and immediately afterwards. The subjects reported that they were unable to concentrate on any topic for long while in the cubicle. Those who tried to review their studies or solve self-initiated intellectual problems found it difficult to do so. As a result they lapsed into day-dreaming, abandoned attempts at organized thinking, and let their thoughts wander. There were also reports of "blank periods, during which they seemed unable to think of anything at all." (Ibid.)

Finally there were hallucinations reported by the subjects while in the experimental apparatus. "In general, where more 'formed' (i.e. more complex) hallucinations occurred they were usually preceded by simpler forms of the phenomenon. Levels of complexity could be differentiated as follows: In the simplest form the visual field, with the eyes closed, changed from dark to light colour; next in complexity were dots of light, lines, or simple geometrical patterns. 14 subjects reported such imagery, and said it was a new experience to them. Still more complex forms consisted in 'wall-paper patterns,' reported by 11 subjects, and isolated figures or objects, without background (e. g. a row of little yellow men with black caps on and their mouths open; a German helmet), reported by seven subjects. Finally, there were integrated scenes (e. g. a procession of squirrels with sacks over their shoulders marching 'purposefully' across a snow field and out of the field of 'vision'; prehistoric animals walking about in a jungle). Three of the 14 subjects reported such scenes, frequently including dream-like distortions, with the figures often being described as 'like cartoons.' One curious fact is that some of the hallucinations were reported as being inverted or tilted at an angle." (W. H. Bexton, W. Heron and T. H. Scott, 1954, p. 74.)

In a later paper (T. H. Scott, W. H. Bexton, W. Heron and B. K. Doane, 1959) the authors show by the use of several tests that "perceptual isolation produces a decline in intellectual ability." (Ibid.) In another paper of the same year (of the *Canadian Journal of Psychology*) B. K. Doane, W. Mahatoo, W. Heron and T. H. Scott found again the presence of hallucinations but they also discovered that the hallucinations occurred developed mainly with those who wore an translucent mask, i.e. that the exposure to diffuse light was a factor in the phenomenon. The authors conclude the report of their work with this general comment: "These results emphasize again the profound degree of disturbance that is produced by the isolation procedure as observed in this laboratory and elsewhere. Hallucinations of extreme vividness, impairment of thought processes, sensory and perceptual changes, together with significant changes in the EEG, all testify to the widespread effect on central neural function that is induced simply by limiting the normal variation of sensory stimulation." (Ibid.)

It is an interesting question what the nature of these hallucinations is and why they occur. It is easy to think of a transitory psychotic experience, if one hears of these "hallucinations" and perhaps that is why they appeared to be so dramatic to some observers. But I see no reason for such an interpretation. I believe one of the subjects defined the nature of these hallucinations quite correctly when he said: I was "having a dream while awake." Of course one could define any hallucination as a "dream while awake," but I believe that one might find such a general definition might not take account of specific qualities of hallucinations, in a psychotic person. I would rather be prone to understand these "hallucinations" as short dreams, in a state of drowsiness, or even not exclude the possibilities that the subjects were asleep for a few seconds and had a dream during this short interval. (The nature of such waking dreams is entirely different from a "day dream." The day dream is not really a dream, but a fantasy directed by certain wishes or fears; the daydreamer is fully aware of the fact that he is manufacturing a fantasy; it can be begun and ended at will and shows little creativity. The dream, including the one a person has while awake, has an entirely different nature.)

It would appear to be a plausible hypothesis to explain the "hallucinations" in the sensory deprivation experiments by the same principle by which we might explain dreaming. In the experiment as well as in sleep the organism is partly or totally deprived of external stimuli and it seems that the brain reacts by creating its own stimuli through hallucinations and dreaming. As quoted by M. Zuckerman and N. Cohen (1964) the same idea has been elaborated in neurophysiological terms by E. V. Evarts, (1962) and by M. E. and A. B. Scheibl (1962). Zuckerman and Cohen quote also other theoretical explanations for the hallucinations in the experiments, namely psychoanalytic, cognitive and social-psychological explanations. Of special interest in our context are the psychoanalytic interpretations. Unfortunately they are mainly tautological: isolation produces a kind of regression; regression furthers "primary processes" and inhibits secondary processes. (Cf. also the later paper by Zuckerman in which he examines the evidence for the various theories on "hallucinations." The author comes to the result that the "sensory hallucinations seem considerably less eerie than when they were first reported by the Canadian students." (M. Zuckerman, 1969, p. 125.)

The authors of the sensory deprivation experiments have pointed out the great general interest their experiments have for the understanding of brain functioning. They write: "There is much evidence from recent neurophysiological studies to indicate that the normal functioning of the waking brain depends on its being constantly exposed to sensory bombardment, which produces a continuing 'arousal reaction.' Work now being done by S. K. Sharpless at McGill indicates, further, that when stimulation does not change it rapidly loses its power to cause the arousal reaction. Thus, although one function of a stimulus is to evoke or guide a specific bit of behaviour, it also has a non-specific function, that of maintaining 'arousal,' probably through the brain-stem reticular formation. In other words, the maintenance of normal, intelligent, adaptive behaviour probably requires a continually varied sensory input. The brain is not like a calculating machine operated by an electric motor which is able to respond at once to specific cues after lying idle indefinitely. Instead it is like one that must be kept warmed up and working. It seemed, therefore, worth while to examine cognitive functioning during prolonged perceptual isolation, as far as this was practicable. F. Bremer and C. Terzuolo (1953) has achieved such isolation by cutting the brain stem; college students, however, are reluctant to undergo brain operations for experimental purposes, so we had to be satisfied with less extreme isolation from the environment." (W. H. Bexton, W. Heron, and T. H. Scott, 1934, p. 70.) Since 1953, a great deal more evidence has shown that the authors were quite correct in the interpretation of their data.

### d) Evidence by dreaming

The phenomenon of dreaming leads us to similar conclusions to those of the sensory deprivation experiments. We take the fact that all of us dream (even though many forget their dreams and imagine not to have dreamt) so much for granted that we fail to raise a rather obvious question: Why do we dream?

Considering that during sleep the activities of the body are reduced to a minimum, except those of the organs that are necessary for the continuation of life, why should the brain not also rest during sleep, since many of its tasks are reduced when the body is resting. Whatever the answer to this question is, the fact remains that our brain is extraordinarily active during all hours of day and night. The fact, now well established by a great deal of experimental work, that we dream during about 25% of our sleep, can by now be understood much better if we consider the need for constant brain activity, not only during our waking time but also during sleep. (The fact that animals even those down to the lower stages of evolution dream shows how fundamental this brain activity is.—Cf. E. S. Tauber and F. Koffler, 1966.) Since in sleep the organism is not accessible to outer stimuli, except unusual ones, it seems that it manufactures its own stimuli in the dream process which have an effect similar to those of the "real" stimuli from the outside world.

But the phenomenon of dreaming shows more than just the brain's need for stimulation and excitation. Many dreams manifest an artistic creativity and depth of insight, of which the dreamers are quite incapable in the waking state. Even the dreams which seem to be entirely motivated by the hallucinatory satisfaction of an instinctual wish (Freud believed that all dreams were such satisfaction of libidinous desires) often show a creative skill in the plot, that the dreamer would not have available during the waking state. Many show an insight into a person or situation, which they are not aware of when awake. An example for such insight dreams is one A had about B whom he had met the evening before the dream. After the meeting A thought B was very nice and decides to go ahead with a certain business transaction they are planning. In the night after the meeting, however, A has the following dream:

"I am walking with B and we come across a river. B, who is a very good swimmer, suggests that it would take too much time to walk to the next bridge and that we can easily swim across. I accept his suggestion, but soon discover that the river has a strong current and I find the swimming very difficult. B has swum ahead of me and when I shout to him that I would rather return he responds with a kind of sneer and swims on. I follow him with great effort and eventually arrive at the other side completely exhausted. B takes my wallet containing important papers and a good deal of money and says: 'I am just going to buy you some medicine.' He leaves and never returns."

When A wakes up from the dream he is shocked. Then he tries to remember the conversation the day before and remembers that he had noticed a peculiar sneering and hostile expression on B's face. Upon further thought he remembers small incidents in the past which would also indicate that B was not to be trusted.—We see that in the dream A had a deeper insight than he has in his waking life. His thought processes in the dream are more active and penetrating than they are when he is awake, and does not respond to the depth of the stimuli.

But the creative faculty during sleep goes still further. Many dreams have the quality of a myth or a short story; in fact, I have listened to many dreams which, if published with no alteration would compare well with Kafka's short stories. In these dreams the dreamer exhibits a capacity for artistic creation of which he shows no evidence in his waking life. The story of the dream is not a fantasy like a day dream; it is the artistic representation of the reality with which the dreamer deals. The dreamer not only sees the truth that is concealed behind the conscious cliches, he is also capable of choosing symbols which express in the most subtle manner what he sees and he furthermore is able to weave an artistic whole out of the various trends of his story.

Let us look at some examples. First a brief dream of a son, age sixteen, who is in intense conflict with his father, an army officer. The son submits to the father partly because he is afraid of him, partly because he admires his strength. One night, after the father had criticized him, he has the following dream: He is at the head of a regiment of soldiers. who are attacking a medieval castle. They breach the walls, kill the defenders and find themselves in the central courtyard of the castle. All the enemy are dead by now; at this point the son discovers that the walls are of cardboard, in fact that the whole castle is similar to a cardboard castle he used to play with as a child.

It is obvious that the dream expresses his rebellious feelings and the wish to dethrone his father and be in his place. But the creative element in the dream is that he chooses a medieval castle as the symbol for his father and furthermore, that this castle is made of cardboard, that it is really a toy and has no strength of power. In this symbol of the "cardboard castle" the dream expresses his view about his father's real nature: he is a romantic living in the past, but instead of being as formidable as he imagines him to be when awake, he sees his weakness, his childishness, his vulnerability. The symbol expresses a quality in the personality of the father with great precision; it is the product of an artistic creation.

According to Freud's principle of interpretation, the dream would only express the wish to kill the father and to ridicule him (the conquest of the castle might be interpreted as incest with the mother). This can be so, but by no means necessarily. The crucial point would be whether the dream describes the real character of the father more adequately than the waking picture. But even if one accepts the Freudian interpretation, the formulation of the symbol remains a creative act.

In other dreams the creative power of the dreamer is not expressed in a literary plot but in artistic visual images; a man, 40 years old, suffering from intense feelings of loneliness and futility sees the following dream image: "I see a street of a big city; it is dawn; no one is on the street except an occasional drunk walking home; there is a drizzle of rain."

This scene is not dreamt in words, but seen as a picture. It is the precise expression of the dreamer's mood in his waking life. Yet, when asked how he feels while he is awake, he would usually give an answer which is by far less precise in describing his mood; in the picture he has captured all elements in such a way that anyone listening to the dream can muster exactly the same feeling of loneliness, of separateness from all others, hopelessness, tiredness.

There are dreams which are variations of the plot of Hamlet. Let us take the plot as Shakespeare formulated it. Assuming Hamlet had consulted a psychoanalyst, what would he tell him? Perhaps the following: "Sometimes I feel uneasy when I am with my mother; I know she loves me, yet I do not trust her fully; and my stepfather—I don't really like him in spite of the fact that he is very nice to me; in fact, he pampers me and gives me many present." The patient then may dream the plot of Hamlet: that his mother together with her lover, whom she marries later, had killed his father.

Is the dream the voice of truth? Not necessarily so; it may be an expression of his jealousy or rebelliousness. But many other times it expresses the truth in a symbolic and poetic form. It does not matter whether the mother actually killed his father; this drastic description may only be the poetic form in which the hidden reality is expressed. This hidden reality is that his mother hated his father; that she is treacherous, unscrupulous, dishonest; that his stepfather is insincere, trying to bribe him, and ruthless. In the Shakespearean drama the truth of the "dream" is established by the appearance of the father's ghost; in life it can be established by increasing awareness of the many details which confirm the dream, sometimes even by discovering not so subtle but concealed behavioral.

The dream in its creative uncovering of a concealed reality, is entirely different from the day-dream which is a fantasy directed by the person's desires or fears. The day-dream uncovers nothing, it just expresses desires. It differs from the dream as a cheap novel differs from a great novel, as entertainment, ideological "art" differs from art. All art—like science but in a different medium—reveals the truth, and does not conceal it. The reactionary artist is a revolutionary, the ideological "artist" (like those following the principle of "socialist realism") has a reactionary function. Homer, in writing the Iliad has done more for peace than those who write "art" for peace propaganda.

Sometimes the same creative power can be seen in persons during a psychotic episode. A patient who spent several months in a hospital during an acute schizophrenic episode was offered clay for modelling. He did a number of sculptures—and destroyed them immediately afterwards. An artist of excellent judgment was invited to be present, and he found that these sculptures were of high artistic value. After the patient had recovered and was sane again he was asked to try modelling again. He did so but produced only very banal cliches When he was asked whether he remembered the sculpture he did during his illness, he had no recollection of it.

A highly intelligent woman wrote me many letters during an acute schizophrenic episode. These letters, while sometimes bizarre, were so brilliant, penetrating and witty that one could have published them without making changes. After her recovery, her letters were very intelligent, as before her illness, but they lacked the extraordinary artistic quality of the letters during the period when she was sick.

It is, of course, very tempting to speculate about the conditions that are responsible for the emergence of active-productive faculties during sleep or during some states of psychosis. In *The Forgotten Language* (1951a) and in *Zen Buddhism and Psychoanalysis* (1960a) I have suggested a hypothesis: During waking life the organism has the function of survival—of producing the goods necessary for survival and defending itself against dangers. That is to say, during waking life man has to work. This means in the first place he has to perceive things as it is necessary to perceive them if one wants to use them. Furthermore, one has to see them as everybody else sees them, since all work is based on cooperation. During sleep man rests; that is to say, he is free from the obligation of work and defense. But this means also he is free from the necessity to perceive the world as it has to be perceived in work and defense; he is free from being impressed by common-sense and common nonsense which influence him during his waking life. He is free to perceive the world in its reality without the distortions of social cliches and purposes. He can see it as he really sees it, and not as he is supposed to see it if he wants to adjust to a group.

It seems that in our sleep (and in certain psychotic conditions in which the adjustment to the world is radically disrupted) as well as under the influence of certain drugs we are free from the influence of the social censors and distorters, and thus free to be creative. One might define the artist as a man who can create while being awake, sane and sober. The sharper the contradiction between social fiction and ideology on the one hand, and reality on the other, the less secret, it would seem, would true insight have to be. In a completely humanized society which does not need to produce the distortion of consciousness, one might speculate that the average person could be an artist while awake. (Otto Rank has the great merit of having shown the connection between neurotic manifestations and artistic expressions, and beyond that, to have made an important contribution to the understanding of the artist.)

### e) Evidence by child development

The area in which almost anybody can observe the activity and passionate interest in what he is doing is that of child development. It is all the more astonishing that Freud and other psychologists did not recognize this fact. Freud went so far as to assume that aggressiveness was originally seated in the ego and developed as a defense of the ego against outside stimuli. More recent research has shown that this is by no means the case. While it is true that the organism of the child as well as that of adults defends itself against an over-stimulation or over-excitation which the psychic system is not prepared to "digest," there is no longer any doubt that the infant, already a short time after birth, is eager for stimulation and excitation and in need of it. David E. Schecter (1973, p. 21) has given a full and systematic presentation of the available data in pursuing his general thesis that "social stimulation and reciprocal interaction—often playfully and not necessarily drive-connected or tension-reducing—constitute a basis for the development of specific social attachments between the infant and others." He quotes a number of important findings on visual perception in infants: those by E. S. Tauber, who has demonstrated the optokinetic nystagmus in newborns (E. S. Tauber and F. Koffler, 1966, p. 382f.); the observation by P. H. Wolff and B. L. White (1965) on the visual pursuit in three and four-day-old infants of objects with conjugate of the movements; of particular importance is the description by R. L. Fantz (1958) that even more in the early weeks of infancy infants prefer prolonged visual fixation upon more complex visual patterns as against simpler ones. "In a loose manner of speaking," says D. E. Schecter (1973, p. 21), "may we conclude that infants 'prefer complex stimulus patterns.'"

Schecter (l. c., p. 23) also reports on the elicitation of the infant's smile which has demonstrated that one can reinforce the smile response by responding with a smile—or tend to extinguish it by failing to respond to it. He refers to a number of recent studies that show that there is "by now a mounting volume of evidence that the crucial variables in determining the outcome of social responsiveness in the potentially healthy infant are the patterned social stimulations and responsiveness of the significant persons in the environment" while without adequate social (including perceptual stimulation) "as for instance in blind and institutional infants deficits develop in emotional and social relationships, in language, abstract thinking, and inner controls."

Piaget's observations of children lead in a similar direction. He observed how the interest of children in the fourth month became "centered on the result produced on the external environment" (quoted in R. W. White, 1959, p. 318). In the second half of the first year, he observed the behavior of the infant exploring the properties of objects and experimenting with various actions upon them. In the case of the nine-month-old Laurent who was shown a variety of new objects, Piaget detected four states of response: "(a) visual exploration, passing the object from hand to hand, folding the purse, etc.; (b) tactile exploration, passing the hand all over the object, scratching, etc.; (c) slow moving of the object in space; (d) use of the repertory of action; shaking the object, striking it, swinging it, rubbing it against the side of the bassinet, sucking it, etc., 'each in turn with a sort of prudence as though studying the effect produced.'" (l. c., p. 319.)

Piaget observes in Laurent at a slightly older age how he manipulates a new object, breaks off fragments, lets it fall and "watches with great interest the body in motion; in particular, he looks at it for a long time when it has fallen and picks it up when he can" (ibid.). He summarizes his experience thus: "He grasps in succession a celluloid swan, a box, and several other small objects, in each case stretching out his arm and letting them fall. Sometimes he stretches out his arm vertically, sometimes he holds it obliquely in front of or behind his eyes. Then the object falls in a new position (for example on his pillow) he lets it fall two or three times more on the same place, as though to study the spatial relation; then he modifies the situation. At a certain moment the swan falls near his mouth; now he does not suck it (even though this object habitually serves this purpose), but drops it three times more while merely making the gesture of opening his mouth." (J. Piaget, 1952, p. 269, quoted in R. W. White, 1959, p. 16.)

White (ibid.) comments on Piaget's findings that "no observant parent will question the fact that babies often act this way during those periods of their waking life when hunger, erotic needs, distresses, and anxiety seem to be exerting no particular pressure. If we consider this behavior under the historic headings of psychology we shall see that few processes are missing. The child gives evidence of sensing, perceiving, attending, learning, recognizing, probably recalling, and perhaps thinking in a rudimentary way. Strong emotion is lacking, but the infant's smiles, gurgles, and occasional peals of laughter strongly suggest the presence of pleasant effect. Actions appear in an organized form, particularly in the specimens of active exploration and experimentation. Apparently the child is using with a certain coherence nearly the whole repertory of psychological processes except those that accompany stress. It would be arbitrary indeed to say that one was more important than another."

To sum up: that children and already the very young infant show need for stimulation and a desire for optimal excitation has been shown by various experiments and observations with children and animals by very competent observers, and thus the older views of the tendency for drive and excitation reduction and the complete passivity of the young infant have been clearly refuted.

## f) Evidence by psychology

While I have thus far presented mostly experimental data, I shall in the following report the views of a number of authors who have arrived at them by patient observation of child behavior and not exclusively by experiments in the narrower sense of the word.

I begin with an exceptional figure in this group, who was not a "psychologist," in the modern sense of the word but a philosopher: *Jean-Jacques Rousseau.* But Rousseau was a keen observer and a brilliant thinker, and ignored today much to the detriment of our own thinking. Seen superficially and out of context, Rousseau seems to share the concepts of man's innate laziness when he describes the savage as one who "only wants to live and to remain inactive." (I gratefully acknowledge this reference to Rousseau and the following quotations to Dr. Hartmut von Hentig and our personal communication.) But Rousseau makes it very clear that this concept of "inactivity" is to be understood only in contrast to bourgeois activity = busy-ness.

"The bourgeois," he continues, "is always active, he sweats, works and torments himself incessantly, in order to provide for himself even more laborious activities. . . . The savage lives from within himself, socialized man always lives outside of himself and submits himself to the opinion of others . . ." (J.-J. Rousseau, 1956, p. 97.)

Or, in *Émile*, he says: ". . . you are worried that the child spends his first years by doing nothing. But what do you think? Is it perhaps nothing to be happy? Is it nothing to play or to run the whole day? Never in his life will the child be so active. Hence, do not get frightened by this alleged laziness." (J.-J. Rousseau, 1983, p. 89.) Or, in Confessions (p. 874) he states: "The leisure I like is not the leisure of a lazy man. . . ; my leisure is the leisure of a child, which is continuously active, without performing anything." If there is any doubt left about Rousseau's position it is answered by the following remark (*Émile*, 1983, p. 117): "Incidentally if the rare case should exist that a child should have the tendency to stagnate in inertia one must not leave it . . . to this tendency, but provide him with a stimulus which makes it alert. It must be well understood that one must not try to force it to be active, but to find something which he likes in order to stimulate himself." Rousseau's statements on the problem of activity are not entirely without certain contradictions; this may be due to certain characterological factors in his personality (like a certain dependency), but the main line of his thought is perfectly clear. (Cf. for a psychoanalytic view of Rousseau's character the excellent doctoral dissertation by Sarah Sue Wittes (1970) which have deepened my understanding of Rousseau.

The same principles made their appearance in the pedagogical system of Montessori, and underlie all recent radical ideas about education, including the most radical one about complete de-schooling of society, as expressed by Ivan Illich (1970). (For the following sketch on the development of the idea of intrinsic pleasure in activity I have leaned heavily on N. Cofer and M. H. Appley, 1963, R. H White, 1959, and J. McV. Hunt, 1963.)

One of the first neurologists in this century to stress man's inner need for activity and stimulation was *Kurt Goldstein* (1939) who on the basis of this fundamental neurological research assumed the existence of one master tendency, that toward "self-actualization," of which the so-called visceral drives are but partial and not really isolated manifestations, and which can find expression in an urge toward perfection—toward completing what is incomplete, whether it be an outside task or the mastery of some function such as walking. More recently *Abraham Maslow* (1954) used this term again and gave it a certain popularity, perhaps at the danger of flattening it out.—Unfortunately in recent years the terms "self-actualization" and "realization of human potentialities" have been co-opted by a popular movement trying to sell salvation cheaply and quickly to all who seek for easy answers. Charlatanry and commercialism characterize many of its practitioners who come up with a brew of self-realization, Zen, psychoanalysis, group therapy, Yoga, and whatever other ingredients are handy. They promise the young greater sensitivity and the older business executives greater ability in "handling" their personnel. Among other regrettable results is the one that serious concepts become dirtied and it thus becomes difficult to use them in a serious context.

In the psychological field, *Karl Bühler* (1924) was the first to speak of the *intrinsic pleasure in activity* and the functioning of the human organism, and called this pleasure "Funktionslust" (pleasure in function). *Henry A. Murray* and *Clyde Kluckhohn* (1952, quoted in R. W. White, 1959, p. 312f.) speak of pleasure in activity for its own sake; they revived

Bühler's concept of "Funktionslust" and came to the conclusion that "the infants mind is not acting most of the time as the instrument of some urgent animal drive, but is preoccupied with gratifying itself."

Among the most important contributions to the concept of intrinsic pleasure in activity is that of *Robert W. White* (1959). In a brief and compact paper he not only gives a systematic review of the various positions sharing the idea of pleasure in activity, but also develops lucidly his own concept of "competence motivation." By competence he refers to "an organism's capacity to interact effectively with its environment. . . ; in the mammals and especially man . . . (it) is slowly attained through prolonged feats of learning." (L. c., p. 297.) White proposes giving the name "effectance" to the motivational aspect of competence. "Effectance motivation cannot, of course, be conceived as having a source in tissues external to the nervous system. It is in no sense a deficit motive. We must assume it to be neurogenetic, its 'energies' being simply those of the living cells that make up the nervous system. External stimuli play an important part, but in terms of 'energy' this part is secondary, as one can see most clearly when environmental stimulation is actively sought. Putting it picturesquely, we might say that the effectance urge represents what the neuromuscular system wants to do when it is otherwise unoccupied or is gently stimulated by the environment. Obviously there are no consummatory acts; satisfaction would appear to lie in the arousal and maintaining of activity rather than in its slow decline toward bored passivity." (R. W. White, 1959, p. 321.)

White summarizes: "Boredom, the unpleasantness of monotony, the attraction of novelty, the tendency to vary behavior rather than repeating it rigidly, and the seeking of stimulation and mild excitement stand as inescapable facts of human experience and clearly have their parallels in animal behavior. We may seek rest and minimal stimulation at the end of the day, but that is not what we are looking for the next morning. Even when its primary needs are satisfied and its homeostatic chores, are done, an organism is alive, active, and up to something." (l. c., p. 314f.)

That the majority of psychoanalysts were opposed to this trend is not surprising, since Freud's whole theory was based on the axiom of the reduction of excitation to a minimal constant level (pleasure principle), and/or the zero level (Nirvana principle). Nevertheless there are a few exceptions to this general trend in psychoanalytic thinking. *Otto Rank* recognized that the achievement of individuation is in itself a creative act; the person who becomes truly himself or, as one might say, actualizes himself—in Rank's terms, the 'artist', has had the courage to overcome his "separation anxiety." *A. Angyal* (1941) stressed the necessity of looking for the general pattern of the total organismic process and accounting for the process of growth. Defining life as a "process of self-expansion," and suggesting that in the process of growth "the general dynamic of the organism is toward an increase in autonomy." Only at the end is the living organism forced to succumb to the pressure of heteronomous forces.

*I. Hendryk* (1943), observing the delight children take in their new-found accomplishments, formulated the concept of a "drive for mastery," a concept that remains within the framework of the Freudian drive theory—but in opposition to Freud's interpretation of children's games which formed one basis for the idea of the repetition compulsion and eventually of the Nirvana principle.

*Ernest G. Schachtel* (1954, p. 318) has stressed that acts of focal attention consist of general sustained approaches "aimed at active mental grasp. . . . Focal attention is the tool, the distinctively human equipment, by means of which the capacity for object interest can be realized." He makes the point that high pressure of need or anxiety obstructs the capacity for such active grasp among children as well as grown-ups.

In my own work since *Escape from Freedom* (1941a) I have emphasized man's need for actively grasping the world and for stimulation. In the concept of the "productive orientation" this need has taken a central place as one of man's basic orientations in the process of relating and assimilating; this orientation of "active relatedness" is the condition for mental health, while its absence, manifested by boredom, constitutes a pathogenic factor, although in milder cases it is compensated by compensatory behavior which prevents the manifestation of conscious boredom.

# BIBLIOGRAPHY

Altman, J., 1967: "Postnatal Growth and Differentiation of the Mammalian Brain, with Implications for a Morphological Theory of Memory," in: G. C. Quarton, Th. Melnechuk, F. O. Schmitt (Ed.), *The Neurosciences: A Study Program*, New York (Rockefeller University Press), pp. 723–734.

—and Das, G. D., 1964: "Autoradiographic Examination of the Effects of Enriched Environment on the Rate of Glial Multiplication in the Adult Rat Brain," in: *Nature*, Vol. 204, 1964, pp. 1161–1163.

Angyal, A., 1941: *Foundations of Science of Personality*, New York (Commonwealth Fund) 1941.

Bennet, E. L., Diamond, M. C., Krech, D., and Rosenzweig, M. R., 1964: "Chemical and Anatomical Plasticity of Brain," in: *Science*, Vol. 146, 1964, pp. 610–619.

Berlyne, D. E., 1960: "Arousal and Reinforcement," in: *Conflict, Arousal and Curiosity*, New York (McGraw-Hill) 1960.

Beswick, F. B., and Conroy, R. T. W. L., 1965: "Optimal Tetanic Conditioning of Heteronymous Monosynaptic Reflexes," in:*Journal of Physiology*, Vol. 180, London 1965, pp. 134–146.

Bexton, W. H., Heron, W., and Scott, T. H., 1954: "Effects

of Decreased Variation in the Sensory Environment," in: *Canadian Journal of Psychology*, Vol. 8 (No. 2) 1954.

Bremer, F., und Terzuolo, C., 1953: "Nouvelles Recherches sur le Processus Pysiologique de Réveil," in: *Archives internationales de Physiologie*, Vol. 61, 1953, pp. 86–90.

Bühler, K., 1924: *Die geistige Entwicklung des Kindes*, Jena (Gustav Fischer) 1924.

Cofer, C. N., und Appley, M. H.m 1964: *Motivation: Theory and Research*, New York (Wiley) 1964.

Doane, B. K., Mahatoo, W., Heron, W., and Scott, T. H., 1959: "Changes in Perceptual Function after Isolation," in: *Canadian Journal of Psychology*, Vol. 13 (1959), No. 3.

Evarts, E. V., 1962: "A Neurophysiological Theory of Isolation," in: L. J. West (Ed.), *Hallucination*, New York (Greene and Stratton) 1962, pp. 1–14.

Fantz, R. L., 1958: "Pattern Vision in Young Infants," in: *The Psychological Record*, Vol. 8 (1958), pp. 43–47.

Fromm, E., 1941a: *Escape from Freedom*, New York (Farrar and Rinehart) 1941.

—1947a: *Man for Himself. An Inquiry into the Psychology of Ethics*, New York (Rinehart and Co.) 1947.

—1951a: *The Forgotten Language: An Introduction to the Understanding of Dreams, Fairy Tales and Myths* (New York: Rinehart) 1951.

—1952a: "The Contribution of the Social Sciences to Mental Hygiene," in: *Proceedings of the Fourth International Congress on Mental Health*, ed. by A. Millán, Mexiko (La Prensa Medica Mexicana), London (H. K. Lewis & Co), New York (Columbia University Press) 1952, pp. 38–42.

—1955a: *The Sane Society*, New York (Rinehart and Winston, Inc.) 1955.

—1960a: "Psychoanalysis and Zen Buddhism," in D. T. Suzuki,

E. Fromm, and R. de Martino (Eds.), *Zen Buddhism and Psychoanalysis*, New York: Harper and Row), pp. 77–141.
—1964a: *The Heart of Man: Its Genius for Good and Evil* (New York: Harper and Row).
—1968a: *The Revolution of Hope. Toward a Humanized Technology*, New York: Harper and Row) 1968.
—1970a: *The Crisis of Psychoanalysis: Essays on Freud, Marx and Social Psychology* (New York: Holt, Rinehart and Winston) 1970.
—1970e: "Humanistic Planning," in: E. Fromm, *The Crisis of Psychoanalysis: Essays on Freud, Marx and Social Psychology* (New York: Holt, Rinehart and Winston) 1970, pp. 77–87.
—1970g: "Epilogue," in: E. Fromm, *The Crisis of Psychoanalysis: Essays on Freud, Marx and Social Psychology* (New York: Holt, Rinehart and Winston) 1970, pp. 190–192.
—1973a: *The Anatomy of Human Destructiveness*, New York (Holt, Rinehart and Winston) 1973.
—1976a: *To Have Or to Be?* (World Perspectives, Vol. 50, planned and edited by Ruth Nanda Anshen), New York (Harper and Row) 1976.
—1989a. *The Art of Being*, New York (Continuum) 1992.
Goldstein, K., 1939: *The Organism*, New York (American Book Co.) 1939.
Harlow, H. F., Harlow, M. K., and Meyer, D. R., 1950: "Learning Motivated by a Manipulation Drive," in: *Journal of Experimental Psychology*, Vol. 40, 1950, pp. 228–234.
Heath, R. G. (Ed.), 1964: *The Role of Pleasure in Behavior*, New York (Harper and Row) 1964.
—1964a: "Pleasure Response of Human Subjects to Direct Stimulation of the Brain: Psychologic and Psycho-dynamic Considerations," in: R. G. Heath (Ed.), 1964, *The Role of Pleasure in Behavior*, New York (Harper and Row) 1964.

Hebb, D. O., 1955: "Drives and the C. N. pp. (Conceptual Nervous System)," in: *Psychological Revue*, Vol. 62, No. 4, pp. 243–254.

—and Thompson, W. R., 1954: "The Social Significance of Animal Studies," in: G. Lindsley (Ed.), *Handbook of Social Psychology*, Vol. I, Cambridge, Maspp. (Addism-Wesley) 1954, pp. 532–556.

Hediger, H., 1952: *Wildtiere in Gefangenschaft*, Basel (B. Schwab) 1952.

Hegel, G. W. F., 1821: *Grundlinien der Philosophie des Rechts*, in: G. W. F. Hegel—Werke in 20 Bänden, Band 7, Frankfurt am Main (Suhrkamp Verlag) 1970.

Hendryk, I., 1943: "Work and the Pleasure Principle," in: *Psychoanalytic Quarterly*, Vol. 12 (1943), pp. 311–329.

Hubbard, L. R., 1950: *Dianetics*, New York (Hermitage House) 1950.

Hunt, J. McV., 1963: "Motivation Inherent in Information, Processing and Action," in: O. J. Harvey (Ed.): *Motivation and Social Interaction*, New York (Ronald Press), pp. 35–94.

Illich, I, 1970: *Deschooling Society*, New York (Harper and Row) 1970.

Kandel, E. R., 1967: "Cellular Studies of Learning," in: G. C. Quarton, Th. Melnechuk, F. O. Schmitt (Ed.), *The Neurosciences: A Study Program*, New York (Rockefeller University Press) 1967.

Karsten, A., 1928: "Psychische Sättigung," in: *Psychologische Forschung*, Vol. 10, Berlin 1928, pp. 142–254.

Ketty, S. S., 1957: "The General Metabolism of the Brain in vivo," in: D. Richter (Ed.), *2nd International Neurochemical Symposium*, London (Pergammon) 1957.

Kleitman, N., 1939: *Sleep and Wakefulness*, Chicago (University of Chicago Press) 1939.

Kolaya, I., 1966: *Arbeiterräte: Die jugoslawische Erfahrung*, New York (Praeger) 1966.

Kortlandt, A., 1962: "Chimpanzees in the Wild," in: *Scientific American*, Vol. 206 (No. 5) 1962, pp. 128–138.

Lindsley, D. B., 1964: "The Ontogeny of Pleasure: Neural and Behavioral Development," in: R. G. Heath (Hrsg.), *The Role of Pleasure and Behavior*, New York (Harper and Row) 1964.

Livingston, R. B., 1967: "Brain Circuitry Relating to Complex Behavior," in: G. C. Quarton, Th. Melnechuk, F. O. Schmitt (Hrsg.), *The Neurosciences: A Study Program*, New York (Rockefeller University Press), pp. 499–517.

Marx, K.: *Karl Marx und Friedrich Engels, Historisch-kritische Gesamtausgabe* (= MEGA). Werke—Schriften—Briefe, im Auftrag des Marx-Engels-Lenin-Instituts Moskau, herausgegeben von V. Adoratskij, 1. Abteilung: Sämtliche Werke und Schriften mit Ausnahme des Kapital, zit. I, 1–6, Berlin 1932:

—MEGA I,3: *Ökonomisch-philosophischen Manuskripten aus dem Jahre 1844.*

—MEGA I,5: *Die deutsche Ideologie.*

Maslow, A. H., 1954: *Motivation and Personality*, New York (Harper and Row) 1954.

Mayo, E., 1933: *The Human Problem of an Industrial Society*, New York (The Macmillan Co.) 1933.

Murray, A., and Kluckhohn, C., 1952: "Outline of Conception of Personality," in: C. Kluckhohn, H. A. Murray, and D. M. Schneider (Edpp.), *Personality in Nature, Society and Culture*, 2nd ed., New York (Knopf) 1952.

Myers, A. K., and Miller, N. E., 1954: "Failure to Find a Learned Drive Based on Hunger; Evidence for Learning Motivated by 'Exploration,'" in: *Journal of Comparative Psychology*, Vol. 47, 1954, pp. 428–436.

Piaget, J., 1952: *The Origins of Intelligence in Children*, New York (International University Press) 1952.

Pomerat, C. M., 1964: *Film: The Dynamic Aspects of the Neuron in Tissue Culture*, Pasadena Foundation for Medical Research, Los Angeles (Wexler Film Production) 1964.

Roethlisberger, F. J., and Dickson, W. J., 1950: *Management and the Worker*, 10th ed., Cambridge (Harvard University Press) 1950.

Rousseau, J.-J., 1956: *Über den Ursprung und die Grundlagen der Ungleichheit unter den Menschen*, in: J.-J. Rousseau, *Die Krise der Kultur*. Die Werke ausgewählt von Paul Sakmann, Stuttgart (Kröners Taschenbuchausgabe Band 85) 1956, pp. 78–97.

—1978: *Die Bekenntniss*, in: Jean-Jacques Rousseau, *Werke* Band 2, München (Winkler Verlag) 1978.

—1983: *Emil oder Über die Erziehung*, Vollständige Ausgabe. In neuer deutscher Fassung besorgt von Ludwig Schmidts (= UTB Taschenbuch 115), Paderborn u.a. (Ferdinand Schöningh) 1983.

Schachtel, E. G., 1954: "The Development of Focal Attention and the Emergence of Reality," in: *Psychiatry* Vol. 17, 1954, pp. 309–324.

Schecter, D. E., 1973: "On the Emergence of Human Relatedness," in: E. G. Witenberg (Ed.), *Interpersonal Explorations in Psychoanalysis*, New York 1973.

Scheibl, M. E. and A. B., 1962: "Hallucinations and Brainstem Reticular Core," in: L. J. West (Ed.), *Hallucination*, New York (Greene and Stratton) 1962, pp. 15–35.

Schmitt, F. O., 1967: "Molecular Neurobiology in the Context of the Neurosciences," in: G. C. Quarton, Th. Melnechuk, F. O. Schmitt (Ed.), *The Neurosciences: A Study Program*, New York (Rockefeller University Press), pp. 209–219.

Scott, T. H., Bexton, W. H., Heron, W., and Doane, B. K., 1959: "Cognitive Effects of Perceptual Isolation," in: *Canadian Journal of Psychology*, Vol. 13 (No. 3) 1959, pp. 200–209.

Tauber, E. S., und Koffler, F., 1966: "Optomotor Response in Human Infants to Apparent Motion: Evidence of Innateness," in: *Science*, Vol. 152, 1966, pp. 382f.

Thomas, H., 1961: *The Spanish Civil War*, New York (Harper and Row) 1961.

Tillich, P., 1952: *The Courage to Be*, New Haven (Yale University Press) 1952.

Verfassung der sozialistischen Bundesrepublik Jugoslawiens, Chapter II, Art. 6 and Chapter V, Art. 96.

Walter, W. Grey, 1953: *The Living Brain*, New York (W. W. Norton and Co.) 1953.

Wells, H. G., 1925: *The Country of the Blind*, in: *In the Days of the Comet and Seventeen Short Stories*, New York (Charles Scribner's Sons) 1925.

White, R. W., 1959: "Motivation Reconsidered: The Concept of Competence," in: *Psychological Review*, Washington 1959, Vol. 66, pp. 297–323.

Wiesel, T. N., and Hubel, D. H., 1965: "Comparison of the Effects of Unilateral and Bilateral Eye Closure on Cortical Unit Responses in Kittens," in: *Journal of Neurophysiology*, Vol. 28, 1965, pp. 1029–1040.

—1965a: "Extent of Recovery from the Effects of Visual Deprivation in Kittens," in: *Journal of Neurophysiology*, Vol. 28, 1965.

Wittes, S. S., 1968: *La Nouvelle Heloise: Rousseau and Authority*. Dissertation, New York (Thesis Columbia University) 1970.

Wolff, P. H., and White, B. L., 1965: "Visual Pursuit and Attention in Young Infants," in: *Journal of Child Psychiatry*, Vol. 4, 1965.

Zuckerman, M., 1969: "Hallucinations, Reported Sensations, and Images," in: J. Zubek (Ed.), *Sensory Deprivation: Fifteen Years of Research*, New York (Appleton Century) 1969, pp. 85–125.

—and Cohen, N., 1964: "Sources of Reports of Visual and Auditory Sensations in Perceptual Isolation Experiments," in: *Psychological Bulletin*, Vol. 62, 1964, pp. 1–20.

# ABOUT THE AUTHOR

Erich Fromm (1900–1980) was a bestselling psychoanalyst and social philosopher whose views about alienation, love, and sanity in society—discussed in his books such as *Escape from Freedom*, *The Art of Loving*, *The Sane Society*, and *To Have or To Be?*—helped shape the landscape of psychology in the mid-twentieth century. Fromm was born in Frankfurt, Germany, to Jewish parents, and studied at the universities of Frankfurt, Heidelberg (where in 1922 he earned his doctorate in sociology), and Munich. In the 1930s he was one of the most influential figures at the Frankfurt Institute of Social Research. In 1934, as the Nazis rose to power, he moved to the United States. He practiced psychoanalysis in both New York and Mexico City before moving to Switzerland in 1974, where he continued his work until his death.

# ERICH FROMM

FROM OPEN ROAD MEDIA

OPEN ROAD
INTEGRATED MEDIA

www.ingramcontent.com/pod-product-compliance
Lightning Source LLC
LaVergne TN
LVHW090607110826
845146LV00001B/288

*9798337209159*